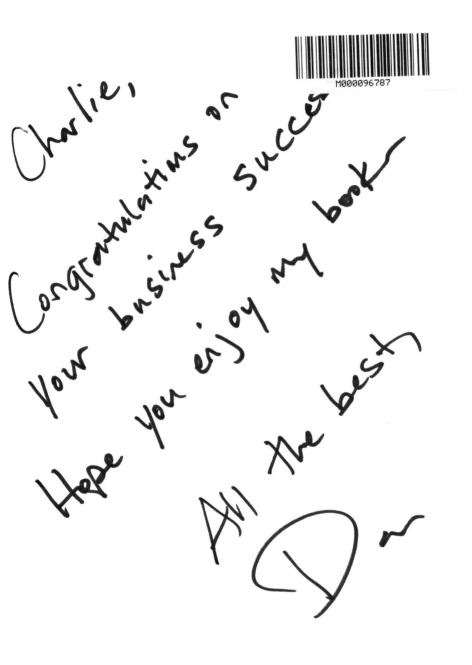

Charlie,

Congratulations on
your business success

Hope you enjoy my book

All the best,

D

ONE WAY OUT

ONE WAY OUT

How to Grow,
Protect, and
Exit from
Your Business

Daniel A. Prisciotta

HIGHPOINT
EXECUTIVE
PUBLISHING

This edition published by Highpoint Executive Publishing. For information, write to info@highpointpubs.com.

First Edition

ISBN: 978-0-9974157-1-1

Library of Congress Cataloging-in-Publication Data

Prisciotta, Daniel A.
One Way Out: How to Grow, Protect, and Exit from Your Business
Includes index.

Summary: "Provides owners and advisors of closely held businesses with unparalleled expertise to understanding the many variables and considerations for successful business exit planning, including retirement planning, income tax reduction, wealth preservation, succession planning and asset protection." – Provided by publisher.

ISBN: 978-0-9974157-1-1 (hardbound)
1.Business 2. Financial Planning

Library of Congress Control Number: 2016947535

Design by Sarah Clarehart

Manufactured in the United States of America
10 9 8 7 6 5 4 3 2 1

Contents

Foreword

By John P. McCaughan

As a business owner your mission is to grow, protect, and transfer your life's work in a way that meets personal and professional objectives. For many business owners, the grow and protect aspect of owning and operating a business is easier than determining who you should transfer it to and what method will provide you optimal financial and personal satisfaction.

Today there is a very large population of business owners who are in the throes of this decision. It is a very complex and emotionally exhausting exercise. There are many reasons why a business owner may be looking to exit his or her business; however, none are more challenging than those faced by the aging baby boomer owner who has reached a certain level of success and is looking to experience the tranquility, peace, and excitement of retirement while ensuring his or her financial freedom and security.

You or someone you know and care about may be among those looking for such an exit, but how do you get there, and who is assisting you in this decision process?

Leading a successful group of financial services professionals who focus on the business owner market for the past 25 years, it has become abundantly clear to me that a process and a coordinated team of competent advisors is necessary to determine and execute the best way to transition and exit your business.

Dan Prisciotta's *One Way Out* provides you with that process, and will take you on a journey of discovery that will empower you to put your plan in motion. This process focuses first on your personal and family goals while quantifying the value needed from your business to meet your life and legacy objectives. It will assist you in identifying the appropriate successor, whether that is a third-party buyer, your management team, employees (ESOP), business partners, or family members.

This is a very emotional and important decision that will have a dramatic impact on the lives of those you love the most. Dan is on a mission to help business owners prepare for what is arguably the single largest financial decision they will face. He approaches each unique situation with great empathy, as well as technical expertise.

It is comforting that Dan, through his years of experience, has captured a well-defined process that simplifies a series of complex decisions that all business owners face as they move towards their own retirement or just have a desire to sell their business. If you are a business owner, read this book and take it to heart. If you are an advisor to business owners, this is a must read that will enlighten you to the difficult financial and emotional decisions your clients are facing as they contemplate their next phase of life.

Reading this book will inform, educate, and motivate you to implement the best approach for you to transfer your business for maximum satisfaction.

John P. "Jack" McCaughan is former managing director, Northeast Regional Planning Group, Lincoln Financial Advisors, as well as cofounder of the Business Intelligence Institute.

My Personal Story and Business Philosophy

I CARE ABOUT SERVING MY CLIENTS extremely well.

I was not born into money but into a working-class neighborhood in the Bronx. My heroes were my father and grandfather. My grandfather was an immigrant who was a printer and often worked nights. My father was the first person in our family to attend college. He owned and operated several restaurants while working toward his degree. Upon graduation, he married, and I was born shortly thereafter. Two more children followed. My mother taught me compassion and love of family.

Through it all, my father continued his entrepreneurial pursuits by starting and running various businesses. Some worked out; some didn't. He always had the courage and fortitude to get up and try again. This tenacity and hard work gene was passed down to me. I consider myself a white-collar guy with a blue-collar work ethic and a deep appreciation that nothing comes free in this world. You have to set goals, create a plan of action, and go for it!

At the age of 11, I started my own car-wash business. My customers were the people who lived in our apartment building. I did not have access to a hose or an electric vacuum. Buckets of water and whisk brooms did the job. Plenty of elbow grease was needed to wax the boat-sized cars of the 1960s and 1970s.

As time went on, I started working in restaurants and catering halls. From dishwasher to busboy, cook, waiter, and bartender, I did it all.

My family and I eventually moved to the suburbs, and throughout my high school and college years, I always worked. During my junior year in college I began a tax return practice and then passed the securities exams necessary to offer investment and retirement services. Yes, it was a very young start in the financial services world.

Unknown to many of my friends, I was an A student throughout my school years and graduated college magna cum laude. Upon graduation, I joined Price Waterhouse and became a certified public accountant (CPA). I learned the language and structure of business but felt limited. So I entered the financial services world to expand my ability to serve clients in multiple ways, in areas such as retirement planning, business succession, employee benefits, and estate planning.

In my financial services career I started at the bottom, doing the tedious internal analytical work—reviewing documents, researching, and crafting the recommendations. I was promoted into management of the firm and ultimately rose to regional CEO of the New York/New Jersey Metro Region of Lincoln Financial Advisors (LFA), with over 100 financial advisors and 40 technical and administrative employees. I learned firsthand how to hire, fire, train, develop, and retain employees. I also learned P&L responsibility, as my compensation was directly tied to performance results.

After 16 years of successful business management, I decided to switch gears and focus my time entirely on serving my own clients. I chose to specialize in the business owner marketplace because of my passion, respect for business owners, experience, and strengths.

To me, success is tied to serving my clients in the best way possible. I realize that I need to continue to earn their loyalty and respect every day, and I never take success for granted. As a result, I am both a thought leader in my field and a lifelong learner. I have become a national resource to LFA and have trained and mentored hundreds of other advisors over my 30-year career.

I am the owner of PrisCo Financial, my financial planning practice, as well as a registered representative of Lincoln Financial Advisors, and a "Prestige" member of Sagemark Consulting Private Wealth Services. I also am the founder and managing partner of Equity Strategies Group, a firm specializing in the design and execution of business exit strategies through a national network of mergers and acquisitions (M&A) firms and investment bankers. I am also the founder of the Business Intelligence Institute, an initiative within Lincoln Financial Advisors to select, train, and support our top 100 advisors to better serve the business community.

I hold American business owners in the highest regard—they are the backbone of this great country. They bring innovation and competition to the marketplace, provide jobs to millions, and make our country the best in the world, despite constant challenges. I am honored to serve my clients and colleagues and take this privilege very seriously. Beyond financial advice, I seek to bring a human element of understanding and urgency to their affairs. I also understand the importance of family and community. I have a large extended family, and our home is often the gathering place for holidays and special occasions. I seek to build and maintain long-term, caring relationships with people I respect and with whom I have the distinct pleasure of serving.

MY BUSINESS PHILOSOPHY: "SERVE FIRST"

The "Serve First" philosophy is about integrity—serving our clients' needs first and last, and always putting their interests at the forefront.

Stuart F. Smith, who graduated from the Wharton School of the University of Pennsylvania in 1924 and went on to blaze a tremendous career as an advisor to many high-net-worth families, first established this philosophy. He addressed the lack of proactive planning.

Smith's "creed" says that many successful people, when it comes to addressing their personal planning needs and wealth stewardship, are "in a mess." He went on to say:

> *Their family and business ultimately suffer from that mess. It isn't their fault. They think they're alright. But someone strong is going to show them the light. I am going to be that person. I will be patient with them. I will inform them. I will concentrate on their problems. I will look them in the eye and quietly, gently, with dignity and singleness of purpose on their behalf and with a good-natured, courteous, persistent intelligence show them weaknesses in their current plans and help correct mistakes they have made. They will receive great personal financial security from my influence on their lives so their family can receive the legacy they have worked so hard to achieve. Armed with logical reasoning I will with every*

decent thing in me, persist, insist, persuade, until they put their financial house in order. I owe them that. I am strong enough to fight for that belief.

I hope that the insights and wisdom in these pages will motivate many to work on their business, not just in it, and learn about the many ways to grow, protect, and ultimately, exit from it. With so many baby boomer owners hurtling toward age 65, a comprehensive plan, including business exit options, is likely to be top of mind. This book and its evaluation of the process will help you to achieve your vision of financial independence by finding your One (Best) Way Out!

Introduction

THE FACT THAT YOU ARE READING THIS BOOK suggests that you own a successful business and care deeply about growing and protecting it. You might even be thinking about how you will exit from your business one day. That day may be fast approaching, or it could be many years from now. Whenever that day arrives, you will want to maximize the outcome—whether you're going to transfer your business internally, to your children or key employees, or externally, to an outside buyer. You have worked too hard to leave this major event to chance. It takes planning, preparation, and near-perfect execution to do it right. There are no "do-overs."

Make no mistake about it: you *will* exit from your business. Everyone does. Your exit is 100 percent guaranteed, whether you go out vertically or horizontally. The only variable is whether your exit will be planned or unplanned. Your legacy will be defined by how well you plan your departure.

What would happen to your business if you were unable to show up to work tomorrow...or ever again?

If you want to achieve an optimal exit, you have important choices to make. Yet it's hard to find objective advice and a well-balanced approach that is tailored to your specific wants and needs. Every owner is different, as is every business. You may have partners, family, and/or investors involved and depending on your success.

WHAT DO OWNERS WANT?

In my previous book, *Defend Your Wealth*, I offered a road map for ensuring the safety of your financial and personal assets in today's volatile world of global economic turmoil, new tax laws and regulations, aggressive creditors, and crafty predators of all stripe. This book is an extension of those strategies, focusing on how to best prepare for the ultimate event for any business owner. After all, exiting your business isn't simply about what happens on the closing date. In order to ensure an optimal exit, you need to know where you are heading and groom your business now to provide for your long-term personal goals.

Today, many business owners want to know:

> "It's never too early to begin this type of planning, but it may certainly one day be too late."

- What is my business really worth?
- How can I grow and protect my business?
- What are the best ways to attract, retain, and reward key employees?
- How successful will my succession or exit strategy be?
- How do I get the most money I can out of my business?
- How much money will I need to live the lifestyle I desire when I am no longer working and taking a salary?
- When will I be financially and mentally ready to exit from my business? How will I know for sure, and what is the process to achieve true financial independence?
- Am I doing all I can to minimize the IRS tax bite?
- How can I achieve my personal objectives, including travel, enjoying family time, reducing stress, and focusing on healthy living?

In my thirty years of practice, I have found that business owners want expert guidance in solving their unique financial challenges so they can achieve their ideal vision for the future. They want a close, personal, consultative relationship with an advisor they trust and who understands them. They also desire the following:

- A complete wealth management experience that addresses the full range of financial concerns. This level of service is possible only when the advisor builds and nurtures a close relationship with a client.

▶ An advisor who can add value, not an "order taker," a slick salesperson, or someone who puts out fires after the business is ablaze.

▶ Simplified financial management. With greater wealth comes complexity. They want someone who can break it down, in English, and create the right plan for them as part of a deeply client-centric process.

▶ Access to required expertise. True advisors to business owners understand the multiple needs of their clients and have affiliated themselves with resources and other professionals who can help satisfy these needs. They bring these professionals in, as needed, on a case-by-case basis to address specific client needs.

▶ Achievement of a long-term succession or exit plan.

In this book I show you how to accomplish these imperatives through a holistic, cross-disciplinary *process*. You will learn how to control the things you can while keeping your eyes open so that you can adjust for future contingencies and opportunities.

THE 5 EXIT PATHS

This book explores the options available now to best position your business for your exit. Part I begins with the 30,000-foot view of why it is essential that you start building your exit strategy now, explains the process of defining your current situation and goals, and describes the

What steps have you taken to exit your business when you are ready?

exit paths available to you. Part II is dedicated to the details of helping you assure that you stay on your chosen exit path—your One Way Out—by growing and protecting your business and your wealth along the way.

This is not an exhaustive textbook, but rather will highlight the most effective methods to get what you want. It is not intended to give you a detailed technical dissertation, but a practical familiarity with the issues and concepts, along with a comfort level that will allow you to ask the right questions of your team of advisors to help you make proactively sound decisions.

The strategies described in *One Way Out* require thorough preparation in order to fully take advantage of their benefits.

So what are these "5 Exit Paths"? There is no "one size fits all" exit solution, but in essence, they look like this:

Exit Path 1: You could transfer your business to family members.

Exit Path 2: You could transfer your business to your partners or co-owners.

Exit Path 3: You could transfer your business to all or a few of your employees.

Exit Path 4: You could sell your business to outsiders in your industry or to a financial buyer, such as a private equity group.

Exit Path 5: You could go public.

All of these are covered in the pages that follow. After examining each one of these in chapter 3, I devote chapter 4 entirely to the most lucrative option: selling your business to an outside buyer for maximum price. This path in particular has great importance to many baby boomer owners today.

That said, I am completely agnostic to whichever path you choose, which is a radical departure from the direction in which many transaction-oriented professionals will try to steer you. My only goal is to educate, inform, and lead.

I confess that I do have a bias for action. Once a particular set of strategies for you are designed, evaluated, and accepted, you should move confidently toward implementation, using a trusted team of professionals to help you do it right.

WHY IS EXIT PLANNING URGENT? WHY NOW?

Exit planning doesn't happen overnight. The correct answer to, "When should I start planning for my exit?" is *now*. Sometimes, you don't get to exit on your own terms, and things happen unexpectedly. People become disabled, or even die. Even if your business is still in the growth stage, you need to deal with unpleasant contingencies that could befall you, your partners, and your key people.

Providing a sense of security for you, your family, your business, and your employees is a reason to create your One Way Out plan well before you determine the date of your exit. Consider what you will do with your time after your exit. Advance planning will help make sure you walk

What is your exit timeframe? Are you doing all you possibly can to position your business for sale at maximum value when you are ready?

away with enough dough, minimize the IRS bite, and prepare for your ideal vision of the future.

If your planned exit is years ahead, be mindful of what can go wrong along the way. There are a myriad of risks. Some can be anticipated and managed. In this book I do my best to identify those minefields and help you avoid them. Once you get past all of that, it is clear sailing.

Financial independence means different things to different people. How do *you* define it? The goal is to find your One Way Out by following a holistic, results-proven process that considers all of your personal and financial objectives, including what's best for your business and, of course, your family's needs. Now is the time to get started.

PART ONE

PLANNING NOW FOR ULTIMATE SUCCESS

Chapter 1

Securing Your Optimal Exit Now

It's a tough world out there—especially if you're a business owner. The landscape isn't likely to improve dramatically any time soon, but there is plenty you can do to ensure that *your* business grows and thrives in this environment, culminating in an optimal exit.

The Great Recession, which began in 2008, hurt most businesses, and many are still climbing out of the hole. The volatility of the global economy, Britain's vote to leave the European Union, along with increases in terrorism, global political strife, and rising budget deficits, have created fear and uncertainty.

There is a growing belief in this country that too much wealth is flowing to the wealthiest Americans at the expense of others, and some want the government to address the problem through higher taxes. Most business owners believe that the focus should be on fostering stronger economic growth *without* raising taxes, which can thwart entrepreneurial spirit.

Our great nation is bankrupt, while politicians and economists seem to have little idea of what to do to resolve the situation. Neither do they seem to have any ability to cooperate with each other to craft a sustainable long-term solution to the national debt, which is approaching $20 trillion. The nonpartisan Congressional Budget Office (CBO) projects that deficits will begin to rise in 2016, and that interest payments will double by 2019, while spending will grow faster than the economy for Social Security and the major health care programs, including Medicare, Medicaid, and Obamacare subsidies.

By the end of 2016, according to the CBO, debt held by the public will be 76 percent of GDP, higher than it has been since the years immediately following World War II!

Global oil supplies are volatile. Europe is also in trouble, and strife abounds in the Middle East. Business owners also face tax increases and tighter regulation, along with the significant challenges of foreign competition, undercapitalization, health care reform, trade deals, and rising fixed costs that threaten margins.

Bad news could send the fragile economy back into a recession, potentially triggering more government intervention in the private sector. That, in turn, constrains business investment, which holds back the very economic growth that entrepreneurs seek, creating a painful catch-22 situation.

These threats combine to assault your personal and business wealth, making it imperative to exert more energy to preserve your independence, security, and stability, and the integrity of your financial affairs.

YOUR PLAN OF ACTION: ONE WAY OUT

Fortunately, you can create a comprehensive plan of action to secure your financial future. You may not be able to exert much change in the global issues I've mentioned above, but there is plenty you can do to grow, protect, and ultimately transfer your business for maximum value. This is your One (best) Way Out.

Your One Way Out plan will require informed, deliberate planning—the sort that cannot be done in a vacuum. It must take into account the whole of your life, your business, and your ultimate goals, considering your personal financial future while defending the wealth you have accumulated so far. (Learn more about this in chapter 2, "Ensuring Success with the One Way Out Process.")

For most of our business owners, creating and implementing an Exit Plan is the most important business and financial event in their lifetime.

Successful business owners will always employ methods to use the tax code and legal system to protect their wealth. They will work hard to grow and protect their businesses and attract and retain key employees in order to achieve company goals.

Still, you need to think beyond those baseline principles, understanding the myriad of risks and exposures you and your business face, identifying the minefields, and planning how to steer around them or defuse them before they blow up.

YOUR BUSINESS AND PERSONAL WEALTH ARE INTERRELATED

Why did you start your business? Freedom? A new idea or improvement on an old way of doing things? Creation of a family legacy? There are countless motivations for becoming your own boss and doing your own thing. High on this list is often the desire to achieve financial independence for yourself and your family. This is the "American Dream" to many. The income you generate from your business creates and supports a certain lifestyle. Various fringe benefits and perks paid by your business protect your lifestyle and provide financial security for the future.

Your business and personal wealth are inexorably connected to one another. Growing the actual value of your business becomes the focal point of true financial independence. There are multiple ways to monetize this illiquid business value, depending on your goals and objectives. It is this liquidity event that will lead to the financial independence you seek. It is critical to plan for the growth of your business, protect it along the way, and properly harvest it, under your terms, when the time comes.

> **Do you have a plan to take your money out of the business on a favorable basis?**

When that day comes, will your financial independence goals be satisfied, or will a gap exist? How do you know for certain? We call this the *value gap*, and it must be calculated and continuously monitored to make sure you get and stay on track.

"Is My Business OK? It's the Primary Source of My Wealth!"

As a business owner, you face a multitude of issues that require you to work *on* your business and not just *in* it.

These challenges suggest the need for sophisticated strategies and experienced advisors to help design and execute growth and protection strategies, wealth preservation plans, and strategic plans for the transfer or sale of your business to achieve financial independence. (See Figure 1.1.)

Oftentimes, the day-to-day, pressing concerns about running your business may dominate your thinking. You're not alone. Business owners everywhere are focused on surviving under the intense pressures of today's economy. They're also concerned about maximizing their value as shareholders and ultimately, keeping their businesses in their families or converting business equity into cash when they exit from their businesses, depending on their specific goals.

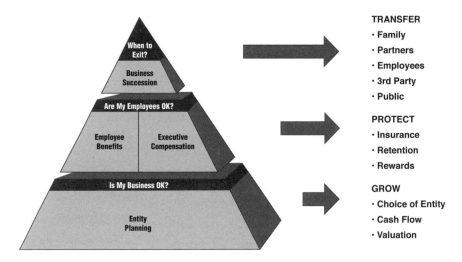

Figure 1.1. Succession planning encompasses the imperatives to grow, protect, and transfer the business.

Do you have a catastrophe plan? What would happen to your business if you or your partner(s) met an untimely death? Do you have a shareholders' agreement (also known as a buy/sell agreement)? Is it up to date? Does the price reflect today's valuation? Unless your agreement has been reviewed in the past two to three years, it may pose a serious threat to you, your business, and your family. Is the agreement properly funded with insurance to give it teeth and make it operative? Without proper funding, the burden of additional debt assumed by you, your partner(s), or the business could be crushing.

As you consider leaving your business, what keeps you up at night?

Similarly, what will happen if the banks call in loans and mortgages that you have signed for and guaranteed personally? An infusion of cash at a critical point in time (such as the death of the borrower or guarantor) can make the difference between business survival and business failure.

How do you attract, retain, and reward key employees? Everyone offers the typical package of 401(k) plans, medical benefits, dental insurance, and so on. You can make a difference by offering special incentive programs to reward long-term retention. This can be an excellent alternative to giving up equity or cash now. These nonequity performance packages can also be designed creatively to align with corporate growth goals and increased revenues and profitability. The better the employee performs, the bigger the payoff will be in the end. These programs can also serve as a sort of "golden handcuffs," in that if the employee leaves before an agreed-upon time frame, benefits will be reduced or forfeited back to the company.

Many additional factors threaten your business wealth as well, including the following:

- Not knowing the value of your business for different purposes, such as, collateral, estate, and gift taxes; future sale; and the like. Planning is difficult if you don't know what your business is worth.

- Lack of a management succession plan. Who will lead your business after your retirement, disability, or death?

- Operational issues. Who will handle the day-to-day operations within your company in your absence? Will key employees stay or go? Issues of compensation, governance, dealing with inactive siblings, and the like need to be addressed.

- Lack of a buy/sell agreement, having the wrong agreement, or having one that is underfunded and can't become operative without potentially disrupting or even bankrupting the business with debt.

- The financial and legal structure of stock transfers to children. Consider the emotional impact among siblings, as well.

- Tax planning to mitigate income, capital gains, and gift and estate taxes.

- Creation of liquidity to pay unavoidable estate taxes due at death and avoid forced liquidation of the business.

- Corporate taxes, a constant threat that hits businesses especially hard these days. Increasing income taxes directly affect your bottom line and ability to create (or just maintain) jobs, provide employee benefits, satisfy lenders, perform research and development, compete effectively, and maintain your lifestyle.

- Increased regulation, compliance requirements, and bureaucratic red tape.

- Insufficient or expensive capital.

- Employee benefit packages that fall out of compliance or become prohibitively expensive or ineffective.

- Exposure of personal and business assets to lawsuits.

"What About My Personal Wealth? Am I OK?"

"Will all of these threats to my business cause me to run out of money, give up my lifestyle, or become dependent on others down the road?"

This is the question we hear day in and day out, at all income and net worth levels (even those with eight- or nine-figure net worths). You need to protect yourself from future threats, such as the following:

- What will happen to me financially after I retire, transfer, or sell my business?

- Standard of living—How much income do I need over the next 20, 30, or 40 years?

- Life expectancy—Will my spouse or I live to age 100-plus? If so, will we have enough?

- What if my net after-tax rate of return in the future is less than it was in the past?

- What if inflation reappears?

- What about the impact of health care when I'm older? Will costs erode my assets?

"Is My Family OK?"

Of course, this consideration is part and parcel of defending your personal wealth assessment. Numerous threats to your family wealth include the following:

- A neglected, out-of-date wealth preservation plan and estate documents. A plan more than three years old should receive a comprehensive review. Inappropriate or outdated wills, trusts, powers of attorney, and health-care proxies can do more harm than you realize.

- Children who are uninformed, inexperienced, and unprepared to handle large sums of money.

- Divorce and substance abuse problems within the family that may affect judgment and good stewardship of your wealth.

- Creditors your children (and grandchildren) may face, including siblings, divorcing and disgruntled spouses, bankruptcies, contracts, or torts (malpractice, slips and falls, automobile accidents, etc.).

- Dying too soon or living too long. A shortened or extended life expectancy can jeopardize family wealth distribution.

- The wrong fiduciaries and a lack of proper successors or trust protectors. These unfortunate conditions place your assets at risk.

- Not adjusting your plans for births, deaths, adoptions, special health needs, or other family changes.

- Lack of liquidity to pay estate taxes. This can result in the forced sale of your most valuable family assets, such as a business or income-producing real estate. Even if your estate is liquid (has cash or short-term investments on hand), the liquidity you stockpile is itself subject to taxes. The challenge is to create a "tax-exclusive" stash of liquidity.

"But I've Had It All Done! I Have Advisors in Place."

Here's a word of caution: Do not fall into the proverbial "I've had it all done" mind-set. I have never met a person whose business and personal wealth defense could not be meaningfully improved or updated in some way. Our clients have found that the difference between merely having their planning work done and having it done as well as possible can save them substantial sums of money, and that's in wealth protected or tax savings.

No single advisor has a monopoly on all of the good ideas, and the rules are constantly changing. Proper planning requires working in concert with experts and advisors, including your financial advisor, CPA, attorney, investment banker, and others, to provide a truly coordinated effort to keep you out of harm's way. The problem is that most advisors don't deliver what you hope they can on their own.

Other impediments to progress come from business owners themselves:

- "These things wouldn't affect me."

- "I just finished going through all of this planning work; I'm sure it's fine."

- ▶ "Who cares what happens? I'll be dead and gone."

- ▶ "I'm too busy or distracted. I'll get to it later."

- ▶ "I hate this stuff."

- ▶ "My situation is unique."

- ▶ "The tax laws keep changing . . . let's wait and see what happens next."

I urge you to become educated, using tools such as this book. An informed client is always the best client.

BUILDING YOUR ONE WAY OUT TEAM

Assembling a team of trusted advisors should be one of your priorities in creating a holistic plan to grow, protect, and exit from your business. (See Figure 1.2.) Think of this as assembling your personal brain trust. Who should be on this team? While each situation is different, here is my suggested list of essential members:

Financial Advisors: Choose a financial advisor who is committed to working with business owners to solve their complex problems. Find one who has the necessary training, support, and access to the multitude of resources you will need to create and execute your One Way Out plan. In my world, we call them *Business Intelligence Specialists*, as they are part of a highly trained national business owner initiative most qualified for this type of planning. Other advisors exist in the industry; just be sure to check their qualifications carefully to make sure they are experienced in working with successful business owners like you. The right advisor can provide the leadership to work through this process and can identify, communicate, and address advanced business and wealth management strategies to allow you to grow, protect, and exit from your business.

Accountant: Frequently this will be your company's certified public accountant (CPA). Select a CPA who has experience in this type of planning and the various tax aspects of growing, transferring, or monetizing a business.

Corporate Attorney: This may be your company's existing attorney, or you may need to seek one who specializes in documenting purchase and sale agreements and other shareholder and employee-related documents.

Transaction Intermediary: An investment banker or mergers and acquisition (M&A) advisor can help you execute the appropriate transaction, if you choose an exit path that requires his or her services. This expert will conduct

Figure 1.2. Assembling a team of trusted advisors should be one of the priorities in planning to grow, protect, and exit from your business.

a business analysis and provide valuation assistance to help develop a possible range of values, as well as find sources of capital or buyers for your business. It is critical to work with the right investment banker for your particular company, industry, and type of transaction. A generalist will not do. Going through a proper exit planning process prior to engaging an investment banker will lead you to an objective, goals-based decision and access to the "right fit" advisor to execute the appropriate transaction for you.

Estate Planning Attorney: Choose an attorney who has experience in planning and drafting documents you will need, and who specializes in executing advanced estate planning strategies for business owners. No generalists here.

Engage your team as early as possible, and make sure they are consistently collaborating on your behalf proactively, not simply responding to your requests.

As your exit and achievement of financial independence draw closer, many decisions will be made—either through proactive planning or passive ignorance—that cannot be undone, so choose advisors wisely.

WHY MANY ADVISORS FALL SHORT

You need to be careful and extremely selective when engaging your One Way Out team. There are many talented and accomplished professionals in every area in which you will need assistance. However, as in any industry, there sometimes

Have your existing advisors discussed exit planning, your preferred timing and strategies to enable this to happen successfully? Or have they been silent?

are conflicts of interest or lack of focus that may create problems with some practitioners—those who may not be at the top of their game in the field of exit planning or don't work well as part of a team. It is these few who make your selection process a little tricky.

Accountants

Accountants are essential to every business. Their core services include the preparation, review, or sometimes audits of financial statements and tax returns, and a variety of other valuable services for businesses and their owners. Having practiced previously as a CPA, I know many excellent people in that field. The vast majority work hard to serve their clients' best interests. However, some are solely interested in keeping you as a fee-paying client forever. Any idea or plan that results in them losing your business for accounting or tax services becomes problematic.

In my experience, some clients have reported finding that financial planning services offered by some firms were not up to the same quality as the core services performed by those firms. The financial planning services seemed like a separate entity, unsupported and on their own, resulting in a disjointed effort.

Some firms may feel threatened if someone gives you advice that they didn't think of first. "If the idea didn't originate here, it can't be good" becomes the mantra of some guarded CPAs. This results in "blind spots" that thwart creativity.

Some present only a historical view. They look at the world through the rearview mirror, instead of looking to the future. Some CPAs are not optimistic by nature. Their training and perspective can make them cautious, conservative, even wary of the future. They tend to focus on what can go wrong, not what can go right. Their eagle eye is trained to seek out problems, breakdowns, and exposure, but not always opportunity. If something goes wrong and they missed the threat, they fear it is their fault.

I had an old football coach who always stuck to his running game. He almost never allowed our quarterback to throw a pass. Why not? "Three things can happen when you throw a pass—and two of them are bad." So, our offense became stale, predictable, and ultimately ineffective, until a new coach stepped in with a different mind-set.

Attorneys

In today's litigious world, you cannot operate a business without attorneys. They can keep you out of hot water, or pull you out if you fall in. Extremely knowledgeable in their areas of expertise, they are needed for legal advice and to draft important documents.

The challenge with attorneys is really not their fault. It's this: You usually only call them when you *really* need them—for example, when a lawsuit has been threatened or filed, a shareholder is getting divorced, you're about to jump on an airplane and want to quickly draft a will or business agreement, or someone has just died.

So why don't you sit down and talk with your attorneys more frequently? Most business owners perceive their hourly (or quarter-hourly) fees to be too expensive for chitchat. "I only call my attorney when it's absolutely necessary. He sends me a bill for every question I ask!" Guess what? Your attorney's expertise and time are his stock and trade. But business owners often want to avoid paying legal fees—even when by doing so they could have prevented a problem from occurring.

Because of their hourly fee structure, attorneys are sometimes hesitant to ask all of the questions necessary to fully uncover their clients' true feelings and intentions. They may sometimes move hastily into recommendations and drafting of legal documents without taking the time to fully understand the issues. Some are not "wired" to ask sensitive questions, or may lack the patience to get into the weeds on what they may misinterpret as "superfluous" non-legal issues.

Financial Planners

Most financial planners want to help but are really investment advisors. Their business model is to provide investment advice and gather assets under management (AUM). Don't get me wrong—investment advice is important. Most investors lack the knowledge and discipline to implement a sound investment strategy on their own. My point is that most financial planners lack the training and support to be much of a resource to business owners. Don't expect the average financial planner to understand or be able to deliver meaningful advice to grow, protect, or transfer your business.

If they purport to focus on business owners, check out their qualifications. Do they have business-owner clients like you, or is their practice a mixed bag of doctors, dentists, widows, and retirees? Do they specialize in working with successful business owners? What services do they offer specifically to this marketplace? Is your financial planner a "lone ranger" or part of a large firm committed to supporting him or her on his or her quest to serve business owners? The smart ones align themselves with firms committed to providing advanced-level training and support, with access to experts—working collaboratively with them to address the complexities that are outside of their practice focus.

Investment Bankers

"When your only tool is a hammer, everything looks like a nail." That's how I would describe many investment bankers or mergers and acquisition (M&A) advisors. They are voraciously looking for their next deal. They get paid a success fee (and initial retainer) to sell businesses.

Once you have gone through an exit planning process, including an extensive analysis of your business and personal well-being and have determined that selling to an outside buyer is the best option for you, then you should absolutely seek out the best investment banker or M&A advisor you can find to represent you and your business. But don't be rushed into a transaction without examining all of your options. Be sensitive to market timing. Is now the right time to sell? Is your business optimized to attract top dollar, or does it need some preparation first? Are you psychologically ready to go? What will life look like after you no longer own your business? How will the sale of your business affect your spouse, children, management team, and other employees? How will your community be affected if the wrong buyer is chosen?

Watch for investment bankers who tell you your baby is extra pretty and build up a false expectation of value. I have seen inferior investment bankers make exaggerated claims regarding what an owner's business is worth in order to get them to sign an engagement letter. It takes months and much emotional agony to later come to the realization that expectations were overinflated.

By then, your choices are limited to selling for less or pulling the plug on the entire process. Find an investment banker who has been thoroughly vetted by your advisors and will work closely with your advisory team to achieve the best outcome for you.

ANOTHER PROBLEM: LACK OF COORDINATION

You may have avoided the pitfalls described in the previous sections, and may already have the very best professionals on your team. However, do they regularly talk to one another about your situation? When was the last time they all sat down together in a conference room for half a day to focus on you and your business situation? Did they work together in a collaborative way to create a well-thought-out plan of action and a way to get it done?

Most business owners I speak with laugh when I pose these questions... because it's never happened! But here's the reality—it's not really the advisors' fault. Who said they should do it? It's not their responsibility. Naturally, you turn to your current advisors to provide expertise to help you achieve your business and personal goals, while trying to avoid costly mistakes and exposure to risk. But here's the reality: Most advisors are very good at performing tasks related to their specific discipline—for example, accounting or law or banking. Many owners express a desire to find that one trusted advisor who can see the big picture, lead the charge, and act as a strategic leader and catalyst to help implement their plan.

Additionally, we often find that an owner may have several different plans (for example, wills, trusts, buy/sell agreements, and beneficiary arrangements) that actually conflict with one another. How does this happen? These plans have been set up at different times, often with different advisors—resulting in an incoherent, disjointed series of actions that lack cohesion and coordination.

So how do you navigate the pitfalls of all of these different financial professionals providing input solely from their own specific viewpoints? What if they lack cross-disciplinary skills or the ability to effectively lead, communicate with, and coordinate the team of specialists required to properly carry out your strategic plan?

LACK OF COORDINATION CAN COST YOU HUNDREDS OF THOUSANDS, AND POSSIBLY MILLIONS, OF DOLLARS OVER YOUR LIFETIME AND THE LIFETIMES OF YOUR HEIRS.

No one advisor can replace all of these professionals (nor is that ever advisable). Nevertheless, the need for cross-disciplinary collaboration with an overall knowledge of how these interrelated areas impact your exit strategy and financial independence plan is imperative.

WORKING WITH A BUSINESS INTELLIGENCE SPECIALIST

Working with a Business Intelligence Specialist—your "advisor of advisors"— will help you negotiate all that has to be done. This person is a trusted, qualified, experienced professional who can go up in a helicopter and review your *entire* situation, both business and personal, and take you through a *process*.

This advisor will bring the strength of perspective to the table. He or she will have worked with many different business owners to develop their comprehensive plan, regardless of their chosen exit path. Such an experienced advisor has seen what works and what doesn't. He or she asks questions no one else asks you, and has certain street smarts, not just book smarts, just like the right CPA, attorney, and investment banker on your team.

This professional also knows how to apply technical concepts to the real world, with access to a deep well of resources, both inside of his or her firm and outside. This expert can crunch numbers to "stress test" and help you choose which option will work best for you financially. He or she will also have the skill set and compassion to understand your wants and know how to carry them out.

A comprehensive, holistic process covering all of the bases simplifies your life and results in the creation of a written action plan that considers the "what-ifs," models your alternatives, quantifies the impact of decisions, and provides a road map for you to follow. Your Business Intelligence Specialist will be able to deeply understand your goals and how all of the moving parts of the process will work together, coordinating and evaluating the progress of your other specialists while providing trusted guidance and counsel for you.

CHAPTER SUMMARY

It's a tough world out there—especially if you're a business owner. We're still clawing our way back from the Great Recession, the global economy is volatile, the national budget deficit is growing. Our national debt is approaching $20 trillion, there are calls for higher taxes, and terrorism is on the rise. All of this isn't likely to improve dramatically any time soon.

Nevertheless, there is plenty you can do to ensure that your business grows and thrives in this environment, culminating in an optimal exit. What do you need to do today to set the groundwork for your successful business exit—your One Way Out? Now is the time to create a comprehensive plan of action, as there is plenty you can do to grow, protect, and ultimately transfer your business internally or externally for the right value.

Your One Way Out plan will require an informed, deliberate process—the sort that cannot be done in a vacuum. It must take into account the whole of your life, your business, and your ultimate goals, considering your personal financial future while defending the wealth you have accumulated so far.

You probably already have a team of advisors—financial, legal, investment—who are helping you manage your business and personal wealth, and these people will be essential to planning your One Way Out business exit. However, not all advisors are created equal. Some are subject to systemic industry issues and conflicts of interest that could come back to bite you. Furthermore, advisors also do not tend to ever sit around a table and coordinate their activities with your overall goals in mind. For these reasons, you need a *Business Intelligence Specialist*—your "advisor of advisors"—someone who deeply understands your situation and goals and can help you negotiate all that has to be done in your One Way Out planning process.

Once you have put together your team, you will be ready to implement your One Way Out plan. Remember that too much talk without clarity of purpose or decisive action is a waste of your time and effort. A leader won't let this happen. Inaction is unacceptable, and the time for you to put your plan into motion is now!

Chapter 2

Ensuring Success with the One Way Out Process

IN A WORLD THAT IS MORE COMPLEX and perilous than ever before, how do you make sense of everything in the midst of all the chaos? How can you best prepare yourself for the important decisions that will preserve, grow, and transfer a business that you have built over your lifetime? How will you achieve, maintain, and pass on financial independence to your family?

It's all about following a results-proven process that anticipates and helps you see your options and solutions clearly!

You are the center of the process. Ultimately, your success is measured by the creation and implementation of a personalized plan that helps you to maximize the probability of attaining your vision, values, and goals.

ONE WAY OUT—WHICH EXIT IS RIGHT FOR YOU?

All business owners will one day exit from their businesses. That's right, 100 percent—either vertically or horizontally. The question is whether you leave on your terms. Will all of your personal and financial goals be satisfied? Will your family be well taken care of? Or will it be a financial and emotional mess?

Everyone exits— either voluntarily or involuntarily (vertically or horizontally).

There are many ways in which you ultimately can exit your business. You may have already spent many years laying plans for one or more of these common strategies:

▶ Gifting or a sale to family member(s).

▶ A buyout with your partners/co-shareholders.

▶ A management buyout, involving the sale of your business to a key manager or your management team.

▶ A sale to an employee stock ownership plan (ESOP). This is an Employee Retirement Income Security Act of 1974 (ERISA) trust that provides significant tax benefits to the company and seller.

▶ Private equity recapitalization—selling all or a portion to a financial buyer, allowing you to take cash off the table and possibly still retain control.

▶ Strategic sale of the entire business to a buyer in the same or a related industry for top dollar.

There are other strategies as well. In fact, there are almost countless nuances and methods for accomplishing this.

However, there is only one way out that is best for you. That one way can be determined only through a process that begins with your specific goals and objectives in mind; that fully understands your business, personal, and family circumstances; that examines and quantifies your alternatives; and that results in an action plan to achieve your desired outcome.

So what *is* your best one way out? Following a process that results in a clear, written exit strategy—one that addresses your need for financial independence and preserves your wealth—will dramatically increase your probability of success. Along the way, you need to calculate and grow your business value, retain and incentivize key employees, and protect yourself. This is the One Way Out process.

Finding your way out is the goal. What is your "best" one way out?

Don't confuse having the ingredients or components of a plan in place with *actually having a comprehensive plan*. To transition successfully, you need to create, communicate, and implement a formal, written strategy.

What you don't know *can* hurt you. Utilizing a comprehensive planning process reduces the likelihood of coordination gaps that drastically and neg-

Whether you are one year or 10 years from leaving your business, the sooner you begin planning, the more options you will have available to you.

atively affect you, your family, and your business. A fully integrated plan includes a process and actions that cover all of the bases, such as financial independence, a business succession/exit plan, tax minimization, risk management, and an estate preservation strategy. A plan also provides a safe environment in which you can test and experience your options before actually carrying them out.

THE "ONE WAY OUT" FOUR-STEP PROCESS

The starting point for creating a plan to determine your One Way Out is a four-step consultative process, as shown in Figure 2.1.

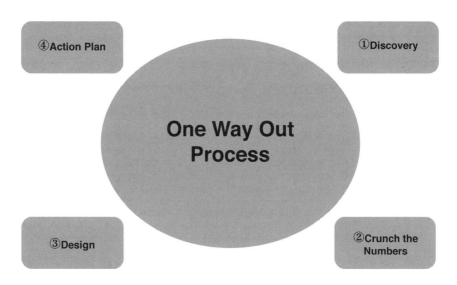

Figure 2.1: Finding your ideal exit plan is a four-step process.

STEP 1—DISCOVERY

This first step in the One Way Out process involves a series of data-gathering meetings in which you share, in detail, financial and personal information about your values and your vision of what you want to accomplish with your life's work. Questions follow a well thought out and ever-deepening sequence. These are not random questions fired out in an interrogation or "let's fill out this questionnaire" fashion.

Ideally, if you are married, both spouses should be present during key meetings. On a select basis, adult children, business partners, and other advisors also should participate. Meticulous records of these data-gathering sessions should be kept and documented for future reference and as a reminder of decisions made.

Decisions can always be changed, but it will be helpful to recall the thought process and value judgments that preceded them as modifications are contemplated. All of this will create an environment in which the most suitable, customized plan can be created to help you reach your business and personal goals.

The Initial Discovery Interview

Not surprisingly, most business owners have done some planning already and have created documents with their accountants, attorneys, and other professional advisors. Like most business owners, you're probably in that group. Still, you may find yourself asking questions such as the following:

- What is my business really worth today?
- How can I grow and protect my business?
- What are the best ways to attract, retain, and reward key employees?
- How successful will my succession or exit strategy be?
- How do I get the most money I can out of my business?
- How much money will I need to live the lifestyle I desire when I am no longer working and taking a salary?
- When will I be financially and mentally ready to exit from my business? How will I know for sure, and what is the process to achieve true financial independence?
- Am I doing all I can to minimize the IRS tax bite?

Does this sound at all like you? Which areas concern you most?

IF NONE OF THESE ISSUES CONCERN YOU, THEN YOU SHOULD PROBABLY CLOSE THIS BOOK NOW.

Assuming you are reading on, let's examine your relationship to your business. This is the starting point of the discovery process.

When I discuss business issues with my clients, I usually find that their business is their most valuable asset. Is that true for you?

Determining Your Mental and Financial Readiness

Before you embark on your One Way Out plan, you should make sure that you're financially and mentally ready for both the process and the end result. Business owners typically fall into one of four quadrants, as shown in the model developed by Pinnacle Equity Solutions (Figure 2.2).

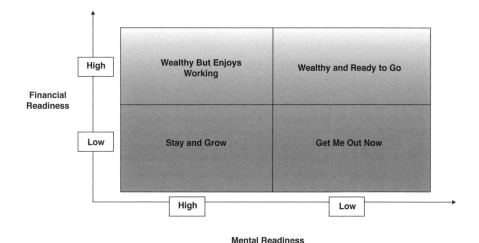

Figure 2.2. Where do you fit in this financial and mental readiness chart?
Courtesy of John Leonetti, Pinnacle Equity Solutions

Which quadrant best describes you? Ask yourself:

▸ Why did you choose that one?

▸ Is there something else you'd like to accomplish? Is there a dream you've yet to fulfill?

▸ What's the most important thing that comes to mind that you would want to make sure is resolved?

Pinnacle also has developed the Business Exit Readiness Index (BERI), a twenty-question survey to help gauge an owner's financial and mental readiness to exit and show which quadrant you appear in on the graph above. To take the BERI, follow the link provided at www.YourOneWayOut.com. It takes less five minutes, and you will receive your results immediately.

Mental Readiness

The timing of your exit, whether via an internal transfer to a family member or employees or via an external sale to an outside buyer, is very personal to you.

Much emotion is tied into this process. It's not just about dollars and cents, which is how it's viewed by the transactional community.

> **Much emotion is tied into this process. It's not all dollars and cents.**

Your business may be an essential part of your identity. It may even be your "baby." Oftentimes it is part of your worth as a person.

Are you ready to move on to the next phase of your life? What does the next chapter look like for you? Solutions consistent with your visions, values, and goals are a critical element to successful implementation of financial strategies.

What makes you tick? What keeps you awake at night? What brings you joy, and how do you define happiness, success, and fulfillment? How will you spend your days when you are no longer active in your business?

With this vital data and intimate knowledge, your financial advisors can help you examine all facets of a proper business growth and exit plan, keeping your best interests at heart.

To help understand your *mental readiness* to transfer or exit from your business, consider the following questions:

When you no longer come to work every day, what will you do with your time?

▶ If **Low** mental readiness:

- What has to happen for you to become mentally ready?
- Are you working your way out of your business being heavily dependent on you to actively run it day-to-day?

▶ If **High** mental readiness:

- What steps have you taken to prepare for your exit now that you're ready?

Financial Readiness

Financial readiness represents your ability to maintain or increase your standard of living from a future cash flow perspective. Will you have an adequate supply of capital and cash flow? Will it exceed your future expenses? Are your current real estate assets, savings, invest-

> **In your mind, how long do you think it takes to prepare so that you can leave your business?**

ments, and qualified retirement plans sufficient? Perhaps most significantly, is monetizing the equity in your business necessary for financial independence?

What is Your Value Gap?

Often you will need significant equity from your business in order to assure your financial independence. The difference between your current savings and investments—including your business equity—and what you need all of that to be worth when you exit is your *value gap*, as shown in Figure 2.3.

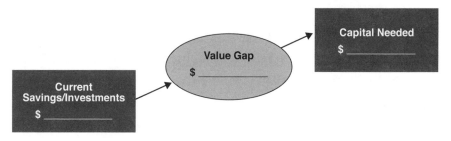

Figure 2.3. Your value gap is the difference between your current investments
and the capital you want to have when you exit your business.
Courtesy of John Leonetti, Pinnacle Equity Solutions

To determine this value gap, you must closely examine your income-producing assets. Many business owners, even those with high net worth, are concerned about their financial independence when facing twenty, thirty, or even forty years in retirement, particularly with current and expected stock market volatility, inflation, health care costs, and taxes that can significantly erode purchasing power and personal wealth.

Examining Your Assets

Remember that one of the objectives of your One Way Out plan is to build a financial model that will help to structure and monitor your financial resources (income and assets) in order to address that value gap and meet your objectives—personal, business, and family—most effectively, particularly with the economic forces now in play.

Here's how you can look at it: You've worked hard over many years, taken risks, persevered, and succeeded. As a result, you have accumulated significant assets (even after paying income taxes). These assets are generally grouped into five broad categories, as shown in Figure 2.4:

- **Business assets:** These include any businesses in which you own an interest, such as C or S corps, partnerships, sole proprietorships, and LLCs.

- **Real estate assets:** These include your commercial properties and personal residence(s).

- **Savings and investments:** Here we're talking about all types of savings and checking accounts, money markets, certificates of deposit, stocks, bonds, exchange-traded funds (ETFs), mutual funds, hedge funds, and so on.

- **Qualified plans and IRAs:** This category includes all types of qualified retirement plans, such as pensions, profit-sharing plans, 401(k)s, SEPs, IRAs, and the like.

- **Life insurance:** You also need to consider all policies on your life (and your spouse's life) owned personally or by a business or trust.

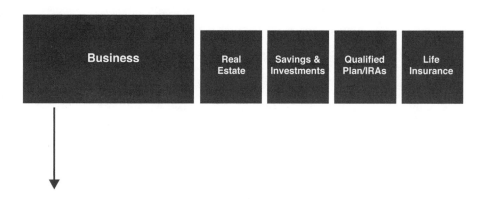

Figure 2.4. You need to consider several asset categories in determining your financial readiness.

The degree of your financial and mental readiness will dictate which exit strategies are best for you. It will help determine your One Way Out. (More on this in chapter 3, "Choosing Among the 5 Exit Paths".) Answers to each of the following questions will help point you down the right path initially.

First examine various aspects of planning for your business. Jot down your answers to the following questions:

- If you're like most owners, your business is probably the source of most of the other assets you own. Is that true for you? What percentage or portion of your personal net worth is represented by your business ownership interest?

▶ What type of entity (C, S, LLC, partnership) is your business?

▶ Are you the sole owner of the business? If not, who are the other owners? Are there any family members in the business or planning to come in?

▶ What formula have you used to calculate the value of your business? For what purpose? When?

▶ Do you believe that your business is adequately capitalized? How much debt is outstanding? Do you need more capital to grow?

▶ How do you plan to grow?

▶ Do you have an exit strategy? Is it in writing?

▶ Which of the 5 Exit Paths will you pursue when the time comes? (More on this in chapter 3.)

- Family
- Partners/Co-owners
- Employees
- Sale to Outsider
- Initial Public Offering (IPO)

▶ Does your company have a buy/sell agreement? If so, how do you know that it will work when or if that agreement is triggered?

▶ What benefits do you offer to all of your employees? Are they competitive in terms of performance, fees, and administration, and are they in compliance? When were they last reviewed?

▶ Do you think your employees appreciate the benefits you provide for them? Are they continually being educated?

▶ If you could improve something about your benefits program, what would it be?

▶ Are you and your key employees able to set aside enough money for the future, given the limited amount of contributions that can be made to a 401(k) plan?

▶ What special compensation programs exist just for you and your most valuable management/executive team members?

▶ Do you offer real equity or synthetic equity to your key people?

- Do you have a plan in place to help you recruit, reward, and retain key employees? What type of restrictions, vesting, or "handcuffs" exist?

- Does your company have insurance to address the loss of you and/or your key people?

- Do you or your company own any life insurance policies for business succession, buy/sell, deferred compensation, or retirement purposes?

- When was the last time these policies were reviewed by someone other than the agent who sold them to you to make sure they are still performing as expected and will provide the liquidity, protection, and cash you need?

- Does the company pay for your personal insurance through a split dollar or bonus arrangement?

- Who is the guarantor of business debt? Will the bank call in loans upon death?

Once you have answered these business-related questions, examine your personal assets. (An overview of these assets is fine for now. You will get into details in subsequent data meetings and document reviews.)

Real Estate

- What is a ballpark value of your real estate (personal and commercial)?

- Is your real estate in your name, jointly titled with your spouse, or owned by your business or other entity?

- How much income does your real estate generate for you?

- Do you intend to sell it? What is your tax basis and potential capital gains tax exposure?

Savings and Investments

- What is the ballpark value of your investment portfolio?

- How are your investments allocated across the basic asset classes (e.g., cash, bonds, stocks)?

- How do you make decisions about where to invest your money?

- Do you feel you are being adequately compensated for the risk you are taking?

▶ Do you know the impact of taxes on your investments? What strategies have you implemented to reduce taxes?

▶ Do you have a written investment policy statement (IPS)?

Qualified Retirement Plans / IRAs

▶ What is a ballpark value of your QP/IRA assets (pension, profit sharing, 401(k) plans)?

▶ What do you plan to do with the assets you've accumulated in your qualified plan accounts—use them yourself or leave them to your family?

▶ Who are the beneficiaries of your plans?

Life Insurance

▶ How much life insurance do you have on your life? On your spouse's life? On the lives of your partner(s) or key employees?

▶ Who owns the policies? (Who pays the premiums?) You/your spouse/children/irrevocable trust/business/partner?

▶ Who is the beneficiary?

▶ When were the tax consequences and policies themselves last reviewed? By whom? What did you learn? Did you make any changes at that point?

Family Questions

▶ Are you married? What are your and your spouse's ages? Is this the first marriage for you both?

▶ Do you have children? Grandchildren? What are their names and ages?

▶ Do any of your family members have special needs?

▶ Are any family members active in your business or expected to come in?

Disposition Arrangements—Wills and Trusts

▶ When were your wills and trusts last updated?

▶ How are they set up? Who gets what, when, and how?

▶ Do you have any special distribution objectives?

▶ Are you currently making any annual gifts to reduce income or estate taxes? If yes, by what amount per year and to whom? Are these gifts subject to gift tax?

◗ Have you done any advanced estate planning (giving away company stock, setting up living trusts, charitable planning)?

◗ What planning have you done to specifically take advantage of the recent Tax Act? Congress is threatening to take away many of the planning strategies available today, so this golden opportunity may be over soon. Have you and your advisors actually implemented changes to take advantage of the latest law?

Is anyone asking you all of these questions? These are just the tip of the iceberg—a starting point to assess where you are at this time. Surely, there are many more questions to ask and other areas to cover, but the answers to these initial discovery questions will provide a sense of direction for future strategic planning. Future data-gathering sessions will provide a deeper view.

Your Document Audit

A critical step in the discovery process includes a review of your existing financial documents, resulting in a summary report that provides, in plain English, an understanding of how your documents actually work. The report should do this both visually and through a point-by-point summary.

Are you confident enough in your current advisors' work to allow another advisor to review your documents? Doing so will provide a "second opinion" and assess what you have done so far to protect your business and personal wealth. It will identify threats, such as financial statement deficiencies, as well as income tax planning opportunities, the marketability of your business, and asset protection. A review of wills and trusts will provide insight into what will happen to your assets in the event of premature death, estate taxes, and so on.

Here are the documents you should review (or have reviewed for you):

◗ Business financial statements (balance sheets, profit and loss, cash flow statements) for at least three years. Also, review current projections, if available.

◗ Buy/sell or shareholder's agreements.

◗ Wills and trusts you created, or those naming you as a beneficiary.

◗ Tax returns (personal and business).

◗ Business benefits programs, including 401(k)s, deferred compensation plans, etc.

◗ Insurance policies and statements, for which you should review ownership and the primary and contingent beneficiaries.

Once completed, this review serves as a summary of your current financial situation. You will have a clearer picture of where you stand financially with respect to your goals, value gap, effectiveness of shareholder's agreements, tax planning opportunities, estate document deficiencies, and potential areas for improvement.

It is often an eye-opening experience to visualize the flow of dollars and understand who gets what, when, and how! The results can be startling, but that doesn't necessarily mean that your financial profile is "wrong." It may simply reflect the fact that your situation and/or tax laws have changed, or other factors have shifted in such a way as to cause your documents to no longer fit your situation and goals as well as they once did. At the end of the process, you may need to circle back to your existing advisors for a much-needed update and revisions or, perhaps, new documents to achieve your desired results.

STEP 2—CRUNCH THE NUMBERS

This is the step where you create a comprehensive financial independence model to help evaluate your alternatives. With this model you can calculate the pros and cons of each strategy in the following areas:

> **Do you know what your business is truly worth in today's market environment.**

◗ The cash flow impact of your possible exit path alternatives

◗ Your business valuation for gift, estate, and buy/sell agreement purposes

◗ Your marketability assessment—the price you could get for your business

◗ Various wealth preservation strategies

Your *comprehensive financial independence model* encompasses your income, expenses, taxes, and direction of your net worth. This model can help you do the following things:

◗ Project your annual cash flow (income and expenses) from all sources alongside your assumed asset growth over the full length of your life expectancy and beyond

◗ Estimate the size of your net worth each year, as well as your savings, your investments, and your transferable estate

- Assess the long-term impact of taxes, inflation, and extended life expectancy on each of the financial strategies you are now using or planning to use

- Consider and quantify the impact of potential threats to achieving your financial independence

This model can help you project and control your financial future, and assist you in deciding whether the course you are following today is prudent or even adequate.

How does the strategy you just implemented, or are now considering, compare with other available options? What might happen if circumstances change (such as differing business valuations, higher taxes, higher inflation, extended life expectancy, or lower returns on your assets, as in the previous example)? The answers might change your mind about the way you've prepared for the future.

A forecast of the next 20, 30, or more years is critical to your financial well-being. On a year-by-year basis, you should project your income from the following sources:

- Salary

- Bonus

- Profits (from S-corps, partnerships, LLCs, etc.)

- Investments (interest, dividends, capital gains)

- Gifts/inheritances

- Retirement plan distributions

- Trust distributions

- Other income sources (sale of a business or real estate, deferred compensation plans, etc.)

A comprehensive financial independence model compares these income sources against your living expenses. Frequently, the most significant expense is the income tax. Are you doing all you can to minimize the cut that goes to your silent partner, Uncle Sam?

In addition to income taxes, consider your personal living expenses, which include the following:

- Mortgage payments

- Real estate taxes
- Food
- Clothing
- Auto payments
- Insurance (homeowner's, auto, life, health, etc.)
- Contributions to retirement plans
- Gifts to help children and/or grandchildren
- Travel/vacations
- Miscellaneous and one-time expenses

Will you be OK? How about your family? How about your community? Under any reasonably foreseeable circumstance, will you run out of money, lose the lifestyle you have worked your entire life to achieve, or become dependent on others? Testing to make sure this won't happen is of paramount importance.

You will not progress to the next step (i.e., sale of your company, the transfer of company stock or other assets to your family, trusts, charitable planning, and so forth) until you are absolutely certain of your financial independence, nor should you. How will you become certain? The best way is to run the numbers. Guesswork or a gut feeling won't cut it. Create a series of financial independence models to analyze your assets, liabilities, income, and expenses to determine whether you will be financially secure years into the future. Don't forget to build in shock absorbers or buffers in the form of different assumptions for inflation, rates of return, taxation, and life expectancy. Stuff happens.

STEP 3—DESIGN YOUR PLAN

Designing a comprehensive, holistic plan involves, well, being comprehensive and holistic. Designing your One Way Out plan is a process of making recommendations and changes to your current situation to achieve your goals and objectives. I frequently refer to the medical analogy of "Prescription without diagnosis equals malpractice." No recommendation should be made or followed without a deep understanding of all of your goals, learned through discovery, and crunching the numbers to model the impact of the recommendations on your cash flow, tax liability, estate distribution objectives, and other important factors. Plan design should encompass, *at the very least,* all of the following:

- **Entity planning, which includes:**
  - Entity selection (e.g., LLC, S Corp, C Corp)
  - Business valuation
  - Assessment of value drivers and detractors
  - Growth and "shock absorber" capital
  - Equity and synthetic equity planning
  - Tax minimization
- **Executive Compensation Planning:**
  - Key person indemnification
  - Nonqualified deferred compensation plans
  - Risk management and insurance arrangements
  - Split dollar and executive bonus plans
- **Employee Benefits:**
  - Profit sharing plans
  - 401(k) plans
  - Defined benefit pension plans
  - Retirement income analysis
  - Group insurance
- **Business Succession/Exit Planning:**
  - Buy/sell agreement analysis
  - Review of cash flow and buyout capital
  - Family transfers
  - Exit planning and sales to outside parties (strategic or financial buyers)
  - Sale of 100 percent of your business
  - Equity recapitalization (sale of a portion of your business)
  - Mergers and acquisitions
  - Raising capital for growth and expansion prior to exit
  - Management buyouts
  - Employee stock ownership plans (ESOPs)
  - Financial independence planning—value gap analysis

◗ **Wealth Preservation:**

- Will and trust design
- Property ownership alternatives
- Qualified retirement plan distribution analysis
- Estate tax reduction techniques
- Trusts created to protect your spouse and children
- Family gifting strategies
- Life insurance analysis
- Charitable planning
- Asset protection
- Need for long-term care as you age
- Multigenerational legacy planning

For details on all of these topics, see chapter 5, "Growing Your Business along the Value Path," chapter 6, "Protecting Your Business with Life Insurance," and chapter 7, "Defending Your Wealth."

A proper design should also address any and all threats to your business and personal wealth. To mention just a few:

◗ For your business, your plan should address valuation, succession issues, retention of key personnel, and effects of contingencies such as death, disability, and retirement.

◗ *All* taxes, such as income, capital gains, surtaxes, alternative minimum, gift, estate, and generational transfer.

◗ Divorce (yours and your heirs').

◗ Liability concerns.

◗ Creditor issues.

◗ Illness or disability.

◗ Premature or just plain "mature" death.

◗ Inflation and potential loss of purchasing power.

◗ Long-term support of family members: parents in need of long-term care or children who can't find jobs after graduation in need of financial support (more prevalent than ever).

- Rising health-care costs.

- Lack of investment performance.

- Improper asset allocation for your stage of life, risk tolerance, and need for income or growth.

STEP 4—EXECUTE YOUR PLAN

This is when you pull the trigger and implement your selected design recommendations. This establishes your One Way Out business and personal action items:

- Prioritize, in writing, the recommendations you are going to implement.

- Assign action items to your advisors (and yourself) to implement.

- Impose a time frame to get things done. Create accountability.

- Follow up and monitor as internal and external changes occur.

Implementing the Plan through Your Business Intelligence Specialist

While development of your written One Way Out plan is an essential step toward the achievement of your financial objectives, it will not be worth the paper it is printed on until you *actually implement it.* (The first three steps in the One Way Out process identify problems, opportunities, and strategies, but do not actually produce results.)

Your plan is not worth the paper it is printed on unless and until you actually implement it.

Effective implementation allows you to realize the full benefits of the work you have undertaken. One of the most important roles your Business Intelligence Specialist can play is that of a catalyst to make the plan happen. Once you and that person make implementation decisions, empower your specialist advisors to carry them out.

Additionally, your Business Intelligence Specialist's roles will be to do the following things:

- Bring creative design ideas to the table in the areas of business growth, protection, and transfer planning. These ideas should also incorporate income, gift, and estate tax savings and wealth protection.

- Coordinate and collaborate with your other key advisors, such as your local accountant and attorney, and bring in other specialists, as needed.

‣ Probably most importantly, act as your catalyst to get things done!

Your strategic One Way Out action plan should be custom designed for you, with all recommendations in writing so that you can follow a well-thought-out road map.

ANNUAL REVIEW AND UPDATE

Creating your One Way Out action plan is not a one-time event, especially in these turbulent times. To ensure that your plan remains current and accurately reflects changes in your business and personal circumstances, tax laws, and economic shifts, you will need to review, monitor, and update your plan on an annual basis.

It is amazing how one year since you reviewed your current plan can become two, five, or ten. I met recently with a high-net-worth individual who had not reviewed his will and trusts for twenty-six years!

When does a plan become stale? Most advisors agree that a plan is stale after just three years. Applying this standard, probably 80 to 90 percent of business owners have stale, out-of-date plans.

CHAPTER SUMMARY

There is a 100-percent certainty that you will exit from your business one day—either vertically or horizontally. That makes it essential to set the plan for your exit now—a four-step process that results in a clear, written exit strategy.

You should not embark on this activity alone. Plan to work with a Business Intelligence Specialist—an extremely well-informed advisor, capable communicator, and relationship manager who brings a wealth of knowledge, wisdom, and experience to the process. Doing so will exponentially increase the likelihood of your customized, comprehensive plan being implemented.

The four-step One Way Out process begins with Discovery, gathering data regarding your vision of what you want to accomplish with your life's work—aggregating and understanding comprehensive, detailed data on your finances, mental and financial readiness, business valuation, net worth, financial forecast, values, and goals for the future. Second, you crunch the numbers, resulting in a comprehensive personal financial independence model and business assessment. The third step is Design—the process of formulating recommendations specific to your situation based on your goals and changes necessary to accomplish them. The fourth step is Execute Your Plan. Implementing your One Way Out Plan is critical to realize the full benefits of the process.

Planning to grow, protect, and transfer your business takes time and commitment. It often requires you to think about unpleasant things. It also will cost money and will need to be maintained and updated. It's essential, and with the right advisors will be worth every dime. Avoidance will only worsen the outcome and could lead to more financial pain and loss.

See the One Way Out Planning Process checklist at
www.youronewayout.com.

Chapter 3

Choosing Among the 5 Exit Paths

THERE ARE GENERALLY FIVE WAYS out of your business. Which is the right one for you?

For most business owners, creating and implementing an exit plan is the most important business and financial event in their lifetime. Whether you are one year or 10 years from leaving your business, the sooner you begin planning, the more options you will have available to you. This chapter looks at the five primary ways in which you can successfully exit your business. By reviewing these and taking into account your own situation and goals, you can choose your One Way Out.

PLANNING AND PREPARATION

At some point in the life of your business, typically during growth or the late stage of the value path, you must consider your ideal exit path. As mentioned previously, everyone exits—either voluntarily or involuntarily (vertically or horizontally). As I describe in chapter 2, it therefore is helpful to understand the key principles of exit planning as a process, not a one-time event. That process takes into account your goals and priorities, the current value of your business and other assets, and your vision of what you want to do after your exit. Once you have identified those factors and have crunched the numbers with the assistance of a Business Intelligence Specialist, you are ready to choose your One Way Out.

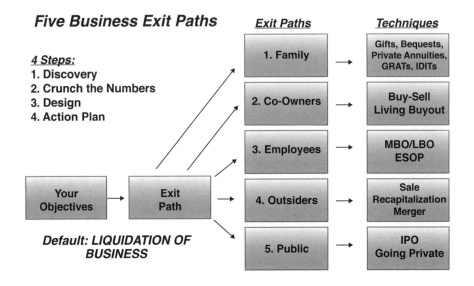

Figure 3.1. Your five business exit paths offer options for your best strategy.

EXIT PATH 1: FAMILY TRANSFERS

Many people find no greater satisfaction than in passing a family business along to the next generation. If children are interested, motivated, and capable of running the business, this is often the objective. This kind of transfer can be executed during your lifetime or upon your death.

If your decision is to transfer your business to family members, it will take years of careful planning to accomplish. First, since this typically is not a liquidity event for the owner (e.g., a sale), you will need to develop other sources of post-transfer income. Second, if your children are going to manage the business, they obviously need an adequate amount of time to develop management and leadership skills. It may be important to retain key people to help with this transition.

The decision to keep the business in the family creates a number of questions, such as the following:

▶ How you will derive an income at retirement?

- How you will provide income for your spouse if you should happen to die prematurely?

- How you will equalize the distribution among children involved, and those not involved, in the active management of your business?

- Ultimately, where will the dollars come from to pay the estate taxes so that the business does not need to be sold in a forced liquidation to pay the estate taxes due?

Planning Priorities

The primary concern is usually to provide for your own financial security and that of your spouse. When considering your objective to keep your business in the family, the main questions are: Can you afford to, and are you and your spouse OK? Therefore, some personal financial planning is necessary:

- **Identify your cash flow needs with a financial advisor:** Create a personalized financial independence model to track your income and expenses. Before you make any decisions, you must run the numbers to see whether the proposed action is feasible.

- **Inventory your financial resources:** Review your assets and liabilities.

- **Evaluate your long-term situation:** Run multiple "what-if" scenarios. If you can achieve financial independence without counting on the proceeds from the sale of your business, then you may be in a position to give it to your children during your lifetime or after you are gone. If, on the other hand, a shortfall exists for you and your spouse without the proceeds, family gifting is not an option. You need to consider an intrafamily sale or other exit options involving a sale to outsiders.

FACT: MANY BUSINESS OWNERS CAN'T AFFORD TO GIVE AWAY THEIR BUSINESSES DURING THEIR LIFETIMES.

Lifetime Gift to Children

Giving company stock to your children is a key consideration when planning to transfer your business within the family. Following are some of the advantages and disadvantages.

Advantages

- Children may be more motivated to make the company succeed with vested equity interest.

▶ Business growth is removed from your taxable estate, and exposure to future estate taxes is reduced.

Valuation discounts (potentially 20 percent to 50 percent) for minority-interest transfers, lack of marketability, and lack of voting control are allowed to be used. Take advantage of valuation discounts now, while they are still allowed under the current tax law. Future tax changes could prohibit the use of such discounts.

Disadvantages

▶ Control/privacy is potentially lost.

▶ Income from business distributions is reduced.

▶ Proceeds are reduced if a parent later decides to sell.

▶ Children assume parents' income tax basis (carryover).

▶ There are costs of valuation, tax reporting, administration of additional entities created (e.g., family limited partnership, LLCs, etc.).

▶ This choice is irrevocable; you can't take it back once it is given away.

How to Give Away Company Stock

You can transfer stock during your lifetime via gifts to family members (or preferably trusts for their benefit) through the use of the annual $14,000 gift tax exclusion ($28,000 if made jointly) and possibly, your lifetime $5.45 million gift tax exemption in 2016, indexed to grow with inflation ($10.9 million if made jointly). Transfers during lifetime, via intrafamily sales, can be structured using installment sales, private annuities, and self-canceling installment notes (SCINs).

Transferring a business to family members can take many forms, including the acronym soup of estate preservation: grantor retained annuity trusts (GRATs), grantor retained unitrusts (GRUTs), family limited partnerships (FLPs), intentionally defective irrevocable trusts (IDITs), and other vehicles. These are covered more fully in chapter 7, "Defending Your Wealth." Take advantage of these techniques while they still exist in their current form. Future tax law changes may greatly reduce the benefits associated with these strategies or possibly eliminate them entirely.

Two-thirds of family businesses do not successfully continue after transition to the next generation due to lack of planning.

Lifetime Sale to Children

If you plan to sell your business to your children during your lifetime, the source of payments and taxation present challenges.

Installment payments may impose a substantial burden on your business, especially when expressed in terms of the sales required to generate the after-tax profits necessary for the principal payments. The portion representing principal is nondeductible for income tax purposes; only interest is deductible.

For example, consider this scenario:

◗ Your company earns $1 net after business expenses and pays it to your child.

◗ Your child pays total income and payroll taxes of 40 percent, which leaves 60 cents.

◗ Your child pays 60 cents to you.

◗ You pay capital gains tax at 20 percent + 3.8 percent (federal and state), which leaves 45 cents of the original $1.

◗ *This method of transfer costs the family 55 cents in taxes on each dollar of value sold.*

If payments continue after the principal's death, the surviving spouse's financial security will be held hostage to the children's ability to continue making the payments.

If an installment obligation remains upon the death of the survivor, it will be includable in the survivor's estate for estate tax purposes, and up to 40 percent will be lost to the US Treasury.

Gift (Bequest) at Death

Another option is to hold on to the business stock until you (and your spouse) die. As previously discussed, this option raises a number of planning issues that need to be addressed:

◗ Grooming your successor

◗ Is someone else capable of running the business?

• What are your distribution objectives?

• What are your projected estate tax costs? Do you have sufficient assets to pay the estate tax, equalize the estate, and keep the business?

If not, what are your options?

- Do you have the appropriate legal documents to achieve this? A will or trust with specific language dealing with the business is needed. All too often, the business is lumped in with other assets.

- Have you taken full advantage of all tax relief and incentive provisions?

- Do you have an adequate amount of properly structured life insurance to deal with payment of estate taxes and equalization of inheritance among children? Without life insurance, all other assets may need to be liquidated, leaving some children with little to no inheritance.

Tax Risks for a Transfer at Death

Transferring your business to a family member is not without risks, of course. Estate taxes are probably the largest impediment to keeping the business in the family. If your business transfers

The day you walk out, the government walks in.

to a surviving spouse, estate taxes may be deferred until the surviving spouse dies, assuming that the owner is married and his or her business interest passes to the surviving spouse, utilizing the unlimited marital deduction.

The objective of retaining a business interest in the family gives rise to several planning considerations that you will need to address. For example, if the stock is to be retained by the surviving spouse, the following considerations arise:

- What will the source of income be for the surviving spouse? If the spouse does not carry out duties commensurate with the salary, upon audit, salary payments likely will be recharacterized as a nondeductible dividend. Further, sales and profitability could decline as a result of the absence of the deceased owner, increasing the risk to the survivors.

- If children are active in the business, conflicts could arise. The surviving spouse will generally prefer security and dividend distributions, while the children may wish to pursue an active growth strategy, often requiring cash and entailing more risk.

- All of the business growth, presumably attributable to the children's efforts, will be included in the survivor's estate. The children will be burdened with unnecessary estate tax on wealth they created.

If your will transfers your business interest to all of your children, you will need to consider these factors:

▸ Inactive family members may own a portion of the business, which could lead to conflict.

▸ You lose the benefit of a trustee to help manage the business.

▸ If you've appointed a corporate trustee who will have no interest in or ability to maintain your business, this may force a sale.

If the stock is to be bequeathed to the active children at the first death, the following considerations arise:

▸ What will the source of income be for the surviving spouse?

▸ Estate taxes may be due upon the stock passing to the children. To the extent that this exceeds the available unified credit, cash will be required within nine months of death to pay estate taxes.

▸ You can transfer only your portion of the business. Any ownership interest your spouse has must also be addressed.

▸ The greater the portion of the estate represented by the business, the greater the likelihood of unequal estate distribution, including possible disinheritance of the inactive children, after estate taxes are paid from liquid assets.

If the stock is to be sold to the active children at the first death, you'll need to take these factors into account:

▸ Any ownership interest your spouse has should also be considered in the sale agreement.

▸ Will the children or business have the cash necessary? If an installment note is required, will the business be able to support the payments, especially after the death of the principal spouse/owner?

▸ Relying on installment payments places the surviving spouse in a vulnerable position.

▸ The sale must be at arm's length; otherwise, a taxable gift may arise.

You must pay careful consideration to where the stock will go upon your death. Does this flow match up with your objectives? If your spouse and your children get along well now, is it important that they continue to get along after you're gone? Will key employees want control of the business and threaten to quit if they don't get it? How will your customers deal with someone else? How will relationships with bankers and suppliers change?

Sale at Death to Children

You may want to plan to sell your business to your children upon your death. This is typically done through a buy/sell agreement, under which the stock in your company is sold to a child or children who desire to buy it in exchange for cash or an installment note to your estate. Life insurance is often used to fund the arrangement. It provides the following:

- Immediate cash to buy stock
- Cash to the surviving spouse
- Liquidity to pay estate taxes
- Cash for equalization or buyout of other children

Considerations

- Will you need to keep and control the business until you die?
- If so, do you have a buy/sell agreement?
- Is the funding sufficient?
- If unfunded, will the business be forced to sell to a third party to pay estate taxes?

Equalization among Children

The problem of equalization arises when you have more than one child and some are actively involved in the family business while others are not. For example, consider the case where a business owner is a widow who dies with three children, with only one who is active in the business. If the business is the most valuable asset and is left only to that child, the estate will be unequally distributed between that child and the other siblings.

This can be remedied through a number of techniques, such as the following:

- Gift company stock to all children, with an agreement for the stock to be purchased later by your active children.
- Gift other estate assets, if enough exist, to equalize.
- Gift nonvoting preferred stock to inactive children.
- Gift nonvoting S-corporation stock to inactive children.

- Create an estate equalization clause in your will/trust.

- Transfer business real estate to inactive children, subject to a long-term lease with the business.

- Use life insurance in a trust to create liquidity to pay estate taxes and equalize inheritances. (See chapter 6, "Protecting Your Business with Life Insurance.")

Timing: Sale of Stock upon First Death

Several timing factors may come into play when selling stock upon your death, but before your spouse dies:

- Any ownership interest your spouse has should also be considered in the sale agreement.

- Will the children or business have the cash necessary? If an installment note is required, will the business be able to support the payments, especially after the death of the principal spouse?

- Relying on installment payments places the surviving spouse in a vulnerable position.

- The sale must be at arm's length; otherwise, a taxable gift may arise.

Creating a Business Acquisition Trust (BAT)

If you are the sole owner of a business, you can consider creating a business acquisition trust (BAT) to purchase business interests from your estate. This trust may act to relieve many common concerns, such as flexibility, gifting of value with retained control, prearranged distribution (control even after transfer), generation-skipping tax savings, creditor protection, liability protection, and divorce proofing. You can transfer stock into the trust during your lifetime (utilizing your unified credit and annual gift tax exclusions) or wait until death to sell to your BAT.

Here's an example using lifetime gifts to a BAT followed by a sale of the remaining business interests at death:

- Immediately gift 2 percent of the corporate stock to the BAT, utilizing minority discounts.

- The remaining 98 percent could be equally distributed between you and your spouse. Each year, you could gift stock equal to your current annual exclusion and/or unified credit amounts to the trust, utilizing minority and lack of marketability discounts (ranging from 30 percent to 40 percent):

- In order to maintain management control, the remaining 98 percent of the stock can be divided into voting stock and nonvoting stock. The portion owned by your spouse, equal to half the value, would be the nonvoting stock, while you retain the voting stock.

- Since you are each gifting a small portion at a time, you may take a marketability/minority discount each time you gift stock to the trust. Therefore, if we assume a 40 percent discount, a gift of $100,000 per year could actually be valued at $60,000 for gift tax purposes. Compare this amount to the current annual exclusion amount. Note that future tax law changes could greatly reduce or eliminate the use of valuation discounts on transfers to family members.

- In addition, you could consider gifting all or a portion of each of your unified credit exemptions (along with the future increases in value) to the trust. In this manner, you could freeze a substantial portion of your business from growing in value inside your taxable estate.

Upon your death, this trust can purchase the remaining shares from your estate. This will do the following:

- Provide cash to pay estate taxes.

- Provide cash to your spouse so that he or she is not dependent on the business for future income.

- Provide trust protection for voting stock.

- Provide management structure to assure continued profitability and fair-market value of the business (trustees and board appointees make business decisions and vote the stock).

- Allow business operations to remain in the hands of trustees and the board until business interests are distributed or the business is sold. The valuation purchase price can be based upon adjusted book value, capitalization of earnings, or another method to pay your family a fair price. The purchase can be funded, in part or in full, through life insurance on you, owned by the BAT.

EXIT PATH 2: SALE TO CO-OWNERS

Selling the business to co-owners is another typical exit path—one that is subject to a whole host of factors that must be carefully considered and woven into your overall plan.

Buy/Sell Agreements

If you have partners or co-shareholders, creation of a buy/sell agreement will be critical to your successful One Way Out. A well-written buy/sell agreement will accomplish three basic objectives:

1. It provides a basis, or a peg, for the value of the business for both a lifetime sale and a transfer at the death of a stockholder.

2. It provides certainty of action by stipulating in exact terms the obligations of all parties to the agreement. It creates a guaranteed market for the sale of a business, in the event of one of the triggering events (death, disability, retirement, divorce, bankruptcy of a shareholder).

3. It prevents company stock from falling into the hands of people who are not desirable as owners, including a deceased shareholder's widow and/or children who are not active or knowledgeable about the business operations.

For the purpose of having the agreement qualify as acceptable in the eyes of the IRS with respect to the value of the stock, the agreement must do the following:

▶ Be for a business purpose. It should provide for effective continuation of the business, create a market for the stock, and so on.

▶ Be an arm's-length transaction. This refers to the situation at the time the agreement is signed, and basically states that it must be between a willing buyer and a willing seller for a price mutually agreeable to both, where neither party is under a prior obligation to buy or sell.

▶ Provide a definite commitment on the part of each stockholder not to sell or otherwise dispose of his or her stock during his or her lifetime without first offering it to the corporation or other shareholders at the stipulated price.

▶ Provide a definite commitment on the part of all the stockholders, binding their estates that they or the corporation will buy and the deceased stockholder's estate, and will sell and transfer the shares of stock owned by the deceased stockholder at the time of his or her death.

▶ Provide a definite commitment as to the purchase price to be paid for the shares that is reasonable and is either of the following:

• a fixed and agreed-upon price per share

• a formula for valuation of the price per share

With the proper planning, you can cost-effectively fund these kinds of agreements, minimizing taxes, through insurance, as described in detail in chapter 6, "Protecting Your Business with Life Insurance."

Types of Buy/Sell Agreements

There are different types of buy/sell agreements. The optimal choice for you generally depends on the tax treatment, post-transfer ownership percentages, and creditor protection issues. The best agreements will address 10 or more triggers, such as the following:

▶ Death

▶ Disability

▶ Retirement

▶ Voluntary termination of employment

▶ Involuntary termination

▶ Divorce

▶ Personal bankruptcy

▶ Loss of professional license

▶ Sale of stock

▶ Transfer of stock for estate planning

Stock Redemption Agreements

This type of agreement requires the entity to buy back the stock in the event of a triggering event. For example, Peter and Joseph are 50/50 stockholders in a business worth $50 million. At Peter's death, his stock passes to his estate, from which the business is obligated to purchase his interest. Let's assume that the corporation planned ahead and acquired a $25 million policy on Peter's life, which is owned by and payable to the corporation as beneficiary. Upon Peter's death, $25 million of cash is paid, tax free, to the corporation. Under the terms of the stock redemption agreement, the corporation tenders $25 million to Peter's estate in exchange for $25 million of stock (Peter's entire interest in the business). This stock is surrendered to the treasury, and Joseph becomes 100 percent owner of the business. All of this is illustrated in Figure 3.2.

Advantage: Joseph now has 100 percent ownership and control of the business.

Disadvantage: There is no step-up in basis for the survivor. If Joseph were to sell the business in the future to outsiders, his basis is still the original basis from when he and Peter started the business many years ago. This exposes him to a potentially enormous capital gains tax at 20 percent, plus a 3.8 percent Medicare surtax, plus any state income taxes due. In Joseph's case, he would lose approximately $16.5 million in taxes. Much of this tax could be avoided through another form of buy/sell agreement.

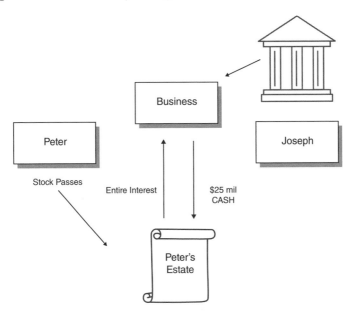

Figure 3.2. Upon a partner's death, you can transfer that person's share through a stock redemption agreement.

Cross Purchase Agreement

Assume again that Peter and Joseph are 50/50 owners in a business worth $50 million and growing. Under a cross-purchase agreement, in the event of a triggering event, such as death, the surviving shareholder is personally obligated to purchase the interest from the decedent's estate. Thanks to the proper insurance planning, Peter is the owner and beneficiary of a policy on Joseph in the amount of $25 million, and vice versa. As shown in Figure 3.3, in the event of Peter's death, the stock passes to his estate. The insurance proceeds on his life are paid directly to Joseph. Joseph then pays cash to Peter's estate, pursuant to the cross- purchase agreement. In return for the cash, Peter's executor transfers the stock to Joseph. The result is the same as the stock redemption agreement; that is, Joseph is the 100 percent owner. (See chapter 6, "Protecting Your Business with Life Insurance," for details on how to arrange for this scenario.)

The big difference between this and a stock redemption agreement from an income tax perspective is that Joseph receives a stepped-up basis of $25 million for the interest he acquired from Peter's estate. It does not matter that the cash came from the proceeds of an insurance policy on Peter's life. What matters is that Joseph, in fact, paid $25 million, and this establishes his new cost basis for purposes of calculating any future capital gains taxes when Joseph sells the business to outsiders.

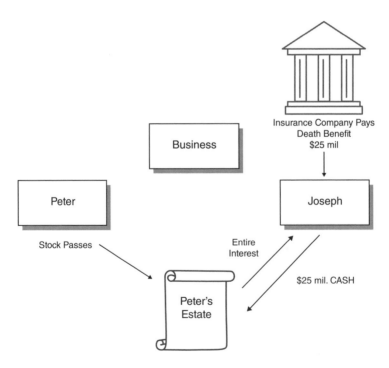

Figure 3.3. Transferring a business share through a cross-purchase agreement offers some significant tax advantages.

Advantage: Joseph has 100 percent ownership and control of the business. In addition, he has a full step-up in basis for the $25 million interest he purchased from Peter's family. If he decides to sell the business later, his capital gains tax exposure on the $25 million is zero.

Wait-and-See Buy/Sell Agreement

Since none of us has a crystal ball and we do not know what the future holds, consider implementing a buy/sell agreement today that addresses all of the possible contingencies while providing maximum flexibility for shareholders.

> **Consider a buy/sell agreement today that addresses all of the possible contingencies while providing maximum flexibility for shareholders.**

With a wait-and-see buy/sell agreement, only one thing is left for future determination: identification of the purchaser. Everything else is put in place, drafted, executed, and defined. However, the identification of the purchaser, whether the entity or the surviving stockholder(s), is left open, usually through a series of rights of refusal. At the time of death of a stockholder, the survivors and their advisors can determine who the optimal purchaser should be. (See Figure 3.4.)

If the tax laws favor a cross-purchase, then that is what will be chosen. If the tax laws at the time of the triggering event favor a stock redemption, then that approach may be taken. This is typically done through a series of rights of first refusal that expire after, say, 30 days and then move to the next option:

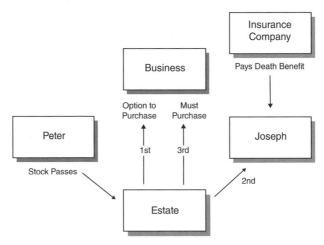

Figure 3.4. "Wait-and-See" Buy/Sell Agreement at Death

- Option to purchase given **to business**
- Option to purchase given **to other shareholders**
- ***Obligation*** to business **to purchase**

Trusteed Agreements

You could also consider the use of a trustee in a buy/sell agreement, which could avoid potential problems in carrying out its terms.

While all shareholders are alive, the trustee can be given the responsibility of obtaining the premiums to pay insurance when they come due, and can also serve as the custodian of the insurance policy, subject to the agreement. (See chapter 6, "Protecting Your Business with Life Insurance," for details.)

Buy/sell Agreement Funding Alternatives

In all buy/sell agreements, certainty of result is important. A properly drafted and executed agreement is the starting point. The final, critical step is to fund the agreement with the proper amount and type of life and disability insurance. Insurance provides cash when it is needed most—at the death (or disability) of a shareholder. Life insurance is typically the least expensive method of funding a buy/sell agreement, assuming shareholders are in reasonably good health. Figure 3.5 shows some sample funding scenarios.

Assumptions	
Current business value	$15,000,000
Original business price (basis)	100,000,000
Percent of business to buy	50.00%
Inflation rate	2.00%
Current gross sales	$75,000,000
Profit as a percent of sales	1.00%
Loan interest rate	8.00%
Loan period (years)	20
Annual insurance premium	104,000
Years premium paid	25

Figure 3.5. A buy/sell funding alternative for 50/50 partners.

Here are the factors to consider when considering funding alternatives for a buy/sell agreement:

▶ **Cash or Surplus**

- Will cash or surplus be available at an undetermined time?
- The government taxes the accumulation of excess cash held in certain corporate entities.
- An active partner may need cash for working capital or loan repayment, and therefore it will not be available to purchase stock.
- The corporation must recognize gain on any assets liquidated.

▶ **Future Corporate Earnings**

- The corporation has an after-tax obligation.
- The corporation's borrowing capacity is decreased.
- The corporation is obligated for principal payment plus interest on buyout.
- The assets of the business become collateral for installment obligations.
- The family of the deceased shares the business risk.

▶ **Borrow from the Bank**

- This has many of the same problems from above but an even higher cost (interest rates) and collateral.
- Fewer banks will make these loans today. Rather, they will likely look to call in outstanding loans when a shareholder dies.

▶ **Insurance Funded**

- The cost is pennies on the dollar.
- It provides the cash while the partners are working.
- It creates a surplus account via the cash value buildup.
- It eliminates the need for the deceased stockholder's family to assume business risk.

Funding Comparison

There are essentially only three ways for a business to fund, or carry out, the terms of a buy/sell agreement:

1. Use the current cash flow of the business to buy out the partner(s) at the time of death.

2. Go to a bank and borrow the money. Of course, you will pay interest on that loan.

3. Prefund the agreement with life insurance for pennies on the dollar. (More about this in chapter 6, "Protecting Your Business with Life Insurance.") These scenarios are shown in Figure 3.6.

Cash Flow (from business working capital)		Borrow (installment note)		Insurance	
Business Cost	$7,500,000	Business Cost	$7,500,000	Business Cost	$7,500,000
Current Sales	$75,000,000	Loan Duration	20 years	Premium	$104,000
Net Profit on Sales	$750,000	Loan Interest Rate	8%		
Net Profit as a Percentage of Sales	1.00%				
Total Payments	$7,500,000	Total Payments	$15,2777,832	Total Premiums	$2,600,000
New Sales Required to Fund Corporate Redemption Buy-Sell	$750,000,000				

Figure 3.6. Typical funding comparisons for buy/sell agreements.

The use of life insurance is often the most cost-efficient way to fund a buy/sell agreement. Using a permanent, cash-value-oriented policy also provides resources for living buyouts in cases where value can be accrued through tax-free withdrawals and loans to buy out a retiring partner.

EXIT PATH 3: SALE TO EMPLOYEES

An exit path attractive to many businesses is a sale to key employees—presumably valuable colleagues who already have helped with the growth and continuity of the business and are important to its future success.

MANAGEMENT BUYOUT (MBO)

Management buyouts are acquisitions of an operating company or corporate unit in which the senior management of the business participates as a significant equity partner in the acquisition. There are different ways to structure this type of buyout. If management does not have the capital to buy you out, as is often the case, you become the bank and will finance the sale by taking back a note payable over a number of years, with interest. (Sometimes, private equity or bank capital can be found with the help of an investment banker. More on this in Chapter 4, "Selling to an Outside Party for Maximum Value.")

A leveraged buyout can be structured to put the debt on the company, not the acquiring management team. Also, an MBO can be combined with an employee stock ownership plan (ESOP; see below) to spread ownership to a wider group of employees and utilize ESOP financing sources.

Advantages

An MBO can often allow the culture of the business to continue and strengthen as employees acquire an equity interest. Other advantages include the following:

1. Flexibility of sale price and deal structure. This could be a fixed price or potential for upside based on performance.
2. Confidentiality maintained to a higher degree.
3. Most of the time, your personal guarantee is removed from bank notes and lines of credit.

Disadvantages

As mentioned, the main downside is that management typically does not have the capital or access to credit to make the transaction happen. Will you get paid in full? The selling party is at risk and may not receive full price for the business. Furthermore, good employees don't necessarily become good owners. You need a willing and capable management team. Lenders will generally require personal guarantees if they acquire company stock. They may not have the tolerance for risk or the entrepreneurial spirit necessary to be successful.

Finally, the US Treasury often takes 78 cents in income taxes in an internal buyout of $1 of business value. The employees must pay taxes on income earned and then buy out the seller, who also must pay taxes. See the example in Figure 3.7.

	Taxes Paid
Buyer: To net $1, business must gross $1.54 @ 35% corporate tax bracket	$.54
Seller: For each $1.00 received from sale, pays 24¢ and nets 76¢	.24
Total taxes paid	$.78
78¢ in federal taxes paid for $1 of business value	

Figure 3.7. An MBO has tax consequences.

EMPLOYEE STOCK OWNERSHIP PLAN (ESOP)

An employee stock ownership plan (ESOP), a qualified retirement plan with vesting schedules, contribution limits, and other Employee Retirement Income Security Act (ERISA) requirements, is designed to borrow money in order to buy stock of a private company and is not concerned with investment diversification. As such, it can be a useful tool when selling your company to employees.

Advantages

Since owners can sell stock to an ESOP on a tax-favored basis and avoid capital gains, it offers many creative uses to explore. If you sell 30 percent or more of your company to an ESOP, you get to defer the capital gains taxes if you roll over the proceeds to qualifying securities. If you hold on to these securities until death, your heirs will receive a step-up in tax basis and never pay capital gains taxes. Other advantages include the following:

- An ESOP provides a tax-sheltered private market for partial shares in a company.

- You benefit from capital gains treatment if stock is sold to an ESOP.

- It offers seller diversification to reduce the risk of having "all your eggs in one basket."

- It rewards all eligible employees with equity ownership.

- It can be especially attractive for an S-Corp, because shares owned by the ESOP can avoid payment of income taxes on profits. This provides tax-free cash to operate the business.

- The selling shareholder can usually retain substantial control over the company and maintain his or her business and personal philosophy even after a company is partially or wholly owned by an ESOP. The ESOP is a friendly buyer.

- An ESOP can protect valued employees from potential layoffs that can result when third parties purchase closely held companies.

- Repayment of the principal of loans taken out by ESOP companies may be made wholly or in part with pretax dollars, which reduces the cost of borrowing for both the ESOP purchase of the shareholder's interest and general borrowing.

> Employees of the ESOP-owned company will have a substantial tax-sheltered retirement benefit that will grow with the company.

Considerations

Take these factors into account when considering an ESOP-based buyout:

> What is the up-front and ongoing annual cost of valuation and administration?

> Do you desire to create a market for your stock without losing control? Shares are owned in retirement accounts, not by individuals directly.

> Are you seeking a method to compensate and reward long-term employees with equity?

> A fairly large and sophisticated pool of employees is necessary.

> You may be able to defer capital gains taxes indefinitely under certain circumstances if your company is a C Corp.

> Often, additional leverage (borrowing) is undertaken.

> Sale to an ESOP will generally not generate the highest price. If your goal is to sell for the highest possible price and become liquid immediately, an ESOP is probably not the best answer.

Figure 3.8 illustrates a typical ESOP-based buyout.

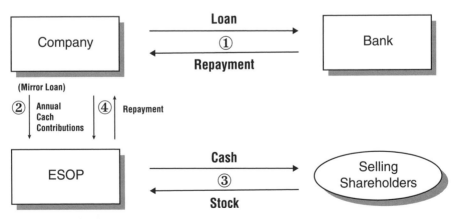

① Bank lends money to company.
② The company lends to ESOP (mirror loan). The loan could also be made directly to the ESOP with a company guarantee.
③ ESOP purchases stock of the company from selling shareholders.
④ Company makes tax deductible contributinos to ESOP. As the Company repays the loan to the Bank, the ESOP releases shares to the ESOP participants.

Figure 3.8. A typical ESOP-based buyout.

EXIT PATH 4: SALE TO OUTSIDERS

A sale to outsiders gives you the best opportunity to cash out at the highest price and sever the risk of ownership. I discuss this exit path in depth in chapter 4, "Selling to an Outside Party for Maximum Value."

The reasons many owners decide to sell to an outside party include the following:

- A desire to cash out and remove chips from the table. Most owners have 80 percent to 90 percent of their net worth locked up in a closely held illiquid business. The prospect of becoming liquid and building a diversified portfolio becomes alluring.

- Fatigue, burnout, or an eagerness to start a new chapter in their lives.

- Decreased tolerance for risk—especially today as the credit markets tighten and banks put pressure on business owners. Personal guarantees become more stressful and put personal assets at risk.

- Spousal pressure or divorce. These have caused more than one owner to sell.

- Unwillingness (or inability) to take the business to the next level.

- The old saying goes, "If the business is not growing, it's dying." What does it take to grow? Often more capital, risk, and hard work.

- Lack of a successor. If the owner does not have children or the children have other business or career objectives, then a sale is inevitable.

- Health issues. A change in health could force a sale.

EXIT PATH 5: GOING PUBLIC (IPO)

Only the strongest middle-market or larger companies may even consider this. An IPO is really a financing tool to grow a business rather than a direct exit plan. In the short term, you may be able to take some chips off the table, but the real payoff may not occur until several years later because of selling restrictions on publicly traded stock. IPOs require a tremendous amount of effort, commitment, and compliance, both before and after going public.

However, IPOs have many advantages, including the following:

- Increased valuation

- Public stock giving the business acquisition currency

- Public stock options used to attract and reward top talent
- Infusion of capital deployed to grow the business further

Considerations

Here are several important factors that should exist for the best results when going public:

- Your company is enjoying rapid growth, with a strong outlook for the future.
- You need capital to maintain momentum.
- The owners do not require immediate liquidity.
- Your company has compelling products or services with proven markets.
- Your company has a strong management team that recognizes responsibility to stockholders.
- Your company has recognized backers (e.g., well-known venture capital investors).
- You are looking to enhance your company's position with customers and employees.
- You will need to address complexity and compliance rules.

Keep in mind that if you are going public, or being purchased by a public company, you may become subjected to SEC Section 16 insider rules, which generally apply to beneficial owners of more than 10 percent of stock. This is an important distinction that requires filings and disclosures in addition to becoming subject to short swing profit rules—a Securities & Exchange Commission (SEC) regulation that requires company insiders to return any profits made from the purchase and sale of company stock if both transactions occur within a six-month period.

Furthermore, if you will be receiving stock subject to SEC Rule 144, selling Restricted and Control Securities, there will also be holding period and trading volume restrictions you will need to be aware of. Also consider any 10(b)5-1 trading plans that may be available to monetize stock holdings in an orderly manner while complying with SEC and other trading rules. It is important to understand what restrictions will be in place.

CHAPTER SUMMARY

The 5 Exit Paths model is designed to help you understand and choose the best One Way Out for you. These paths are:

- **Sale to family members:** Family succession requires years of careful planning to execute successfully. Decisions such as giving stock to children, selling to them during life, or bequeathing at death need to be addressed. Equalization among inactive children, timing, and tax planning are crucial.

- **Sale to co-owners:** Buy/sell agreements are needed to protect you, your family, and your co-shareholders while ensuring continuity of the business. Proper design and insurance funding are necessary.

- **Sale to employees:** Identification of a strong management team with the financial wherewithal is the first step on this path. Structuring of the sale to minimize taxes and provide you with security of receiving payments comes next.

- **Sale to outside buyers:** A sale to outsiders yields the highest price. (The next chapter will address the key steps in this process.)

- **A public offering (IPO):** The IPO is losing popularity today. Only the largest companies can consider doing so.

Understand your options and work with your business intelligence advisor to implement strategies that enable you to exit your business on your own terms, at the most appropriate time, with minimal tax consequences, and at the right value.

Move quickly to take advantage of strategies available under current tax laws before they are taken away. Be proactive in developing your exit plan. Create a comprehensive financial independence plan to help meet your long-term goals of financial security and preservation of wealth for your family.

Your plan should include a financial independence model before you commit to an exit path, in order to help do the following:

- Provide a long-term perspective

- Demonstrate various what-if scenarios at different values and evaluate your net cash flows after you transfer or sell your business

- Prepare for your future after the business transition is complete

- Consider presale planning strategies to reduce income and estate taxes

The bottom line for all of this: Don't put off exit planning!

Chapter 4

Selling to an Outside Party for Maximum Value

YOU HAVE WORKED EXTREMELY HARD to build your business into the successful enterprise it is today. After careful examination of your possible exit paths, number crunching, and thinking about your future, you have chosen Exit Path 4: Selling your business to an outside buyer. In the vast majority of cases, this is the preferred exit strategy to maximize the value of your business, create liquidity, and sever risk.

Timing is critical. Business and economic factors, some of which are beyond your control, could change. When the financial crisis struck in 2008, owners who had been contemplating their exit were stuck because the values of nearly every type of business were negatively affected. Liquidity disappeared from the marketplace, and even interested buyers had extreme difficulties obtaining financing. Any business owners who had put off mapping out and executing an exit strategy were basically out of luck for the next four or five years while the financial crisis and resulting recession ran their course.

> **How will you make sure you get maximum value and terms for the sale of your business?**

Even when the economy began to recover from the recession, business values were still suppressed, financing remained difficult, and potential buyers were skittish. The lesson learned here is that you can't put off implementing your exit strategy; if you do, you might have to wait four, five, or even six years for the market recovery—a time luxury that you may not have.

Now is when you need to prepare yourself and your business for the sale, but how do you sell for maximum value? The answer can be found in a results-proven process, combined with working with top advisors who can bring you all the way home.

YOU NEED AN EXPERT

You should not try to sell your business on your own, since it is a complex process fraught with land mines. As an entrepreneur, I realize the temptation to try to sell on your own may be strong. After all, who knows your business and your industry better than you? However, selling a business takes a specific skill set learned over many years of experience in dealing with buyers and sellers. Moreover, your emotional attachment to your business may make it difficult, if not impossible, to negotiate with potential buyers in an objective, dispassionate way. Experienced buyers are pros at buying companies, and negotiations will get intense.

THE STAKES ARE HIGH, AND YOU DON'T GET A SECOND CHANCE TO DO IT RIGHT.

Professional transaction intermediaries, including mergers and acquisitions (M&A) advisors and investment bankers, focus 100 percent of their time and effort on selling businesses like yours for maximum value.

Working with an M&A advisor or investment banker will assist you in the following areas:

- Access to additional premium buyers, both strategic and private equity buyers, with deep pockets to execute the transaction.

- Planning and executing your sales strategy. The investment banker may take a rifle approach and target just a few highly qualified potential buyers, or a shotgun approach to expose your business to many suitors. In either case, confidentiality will be maintained throughout the process, and you will discuss and agree on the specific approach up front.

- Assuring that you maintain control of the process and final decisions, with the efficiency of not having to administer the details of the day-to-day marketing and selling of your business.

• Creating a competitive auction in which multiple potential buyers, having identical information, simultaneously bid to buy your company. Any owner would be hard pressed to find and deal with more than one buyer at a time. Even if you have already received an unsolicited offer, it would be best to insert an investment banker into the equation to orchestrate, negotiate, manage the process, and ensure the deal actually closes. You can jump in at the appropriate time to break a deadlock as the final decision maker (or to play good cop, bad cop). This "political capital" loses potency if you are too close to the deal throughout the process.

• Minimizing disruption to your business. The last thing you want to do is take your eye off the ball and allow your business to skid during the selling process. A potential buyer will exploit that to drastically reduce price or terms, leading to less cash at closing and more deferred through a note or earn-out.

CASE STUDY

This case study showcases the strengths of Equity Strategies Group (ESG), where we help the owners of privately held businesses plan for and implement a successful exit strategy. For most business owners, this is a once-in-a-lifetime event and one of the most important decisions they will ever make.

In this case the owner, after completing our exit planning process and analyzing the various exit paths with his financial advisor, made an informed decision to sell his business to an outside party. His objective was to achieve the highest possible selling price. For him, this was his preferred One Way Out. His financial advisor consulted with ESG and together we selected the "best fit" M&A firm to represent him.

"Fortunately, I am not one of those business owners who made a multimillion-dollar mistake by thinking I could sell my company without the assistance of an M&A advisor. My M&A advisor helped me realize the true value of my company and designed a process to result in the best outcome for me. I am extremely thankful for the professional advice and guidance I received throughout the sale process, which in

the end yielded a transaction value well beyond what I had initially imagined possible."

The quote above is from the owner whose service business was recently sold. It is with good reason that he professes his thankfulness to his advisory team: *We sold his business for 82.3 times the company's* past 12-month EBITDA and 13 times the following year's projected EBITDA—*an unheard-of multiple in any industry.* Several factors were leveraged in the transaction to result in such an unbelievable value for the client's company. What follows is a case study of the process and transaction we facilitated for this owner.

The company was about five years old and growing rapidly in the medical services field. It was competing with a handful of much larger publicly owned companies. The client realized that in order to continue on its growth trajectory, the company would need the infusion of substantial and much-needed working capital in the range of $4 million to $6 million. The client had planned from the beginning to build the business for an eventual sale, but he felt that it was still too early in the building process to take that step. He believed that his company's revenues and profits had not yet reached the levels that traditional valuation models suggested could result in a transaction sizable enough to satisfy his objectives and help him achieve financial independence.

At this point, the client's financial advisors at Sagemark Consulting introduced ESG to evaluate the business and help the company satisfy its working capital needs and exit strategy.

ESG began the process of capital raising and presale planning by initially conducting a series of interviews with the business owner to clearly establish objectives, gain a deeper understanding of the business and industry, and create a *marketability assessment.* This assessment is the result of financial statement analysis (three years of corporate balance sheets and profit-and-loss statements) and in-depth questioning of the business owner to truly understand his company and various value drivers that either enhance or detract from enterprise value. It also involved research of the industry, values of similar businesses, and knowledge of prevailing EBITDA multiples.

You would be amazed by what can be accomplished through teleconferences, videoconferences, and the Internet. In this case, technology enabled ESG to ask the owner questions about the major factors that would affect the sale of the business (explained further in this chapter), assess the business, establish capital needs, and develop a range of market values for the business (which greatly exceeded the owner's estimate of the value of his business). Ultimately, ESG introduced the owner to several highly qualified M&A advisory firms in its national network. The choice of firms was made on the basis of several important criteria:

- Industry expertise (medical devices, in this case)
- Type of transaction desired (capital raising, leading to a sale of the business, either 100 percent or partial sale through an equity recapitalization)
- Size of the transactions proposed (You don't want an M&A advisor that is either too big or too small to meet your needs, but rather a fit that is "just right," with a firm that will provide senior-level attention to your business.)
- Personality and chemistry of parties involved
- Finally, geography (because the firms chosen had multiple offices near the client's location, working together was convenient and cost-effective)

After interviewing several of ESG's M&A candidates, the owner chose the regional office of an internationally respected and seasoned M&A advisory firm to represent his company. After reviewing the company at length, the M&A advisor agreed that it might be worth much more than the owner had anticipated. This was due in part to the company's high growth rate, knowledge capital, systems and processes in place, and geographic competitive advantage. A two-pronged plan was implemented: working capital would be sought while at the same time feelers would be put out to a handful of private equity groups (PEGs) and synergistic companies to get an idea of market interest in an outright acquisition.

Initially, the outreach was to traditional funding sources, consisting primarily of companies that specialized in higher-risk capital such as mezzanine and PEGs. The client was thrilled by the strong response level he received. However, upon carefully reviewing the proposals that came in from this initial outreach, the client realized that he would have to give up more equity than desired in order to obtain the amount of working capital preferred. This is where the situation started to get very exciting.

After consulting with the owner, the team decided to focus more intently on the possibility of an outright sale of the company. Some of the PEGs initially contacted as funding sources had expressed an interest in an outright or majority purchase. Follow-ups would be scheduled to initiate further dialogue about that possibility.

Additionally, the client was aware of at least one other large synergistic company that had an interest in entering the space. That company was contacted to open a dialogue about the possibility of utilizing the client's company as its platform for entrance into the market space. Both of these avenues could be explored without tipping off the industry competitors as to the client's intentions, and this is exactly how the process unfolded.

Similar to the intense interest received while seeking proposals to satisfy the company's working capital needs, the opportunity for an outright acquisition of the client's company resulted in equally heated competition. Proposals were submitted by quite a few PEGs, as well as from a synergistic company looking to enter the space. These opening proposals, although varying to great degrees in their value propositions, all fell inside the range of what would be considered the market value of the company, based on generally accepted valuation metrics. It was now time for the M&A firm to earn its fee.

At this point, the M&A advisor put together a valuation package to share with the PEGs and the synergistic company that were vying to purchase the business.

The results were well beyond expectations. The analysis estimated the value of the company to a PEG industry competitor and on a discounted future-earnings basis. All methodologies employed in the analysis were based on solid assumptions but pushed the envelope a bit on traditional thinking. As a result, the company's range of values derived in the analysis was far in excess of the offers previously submitted by the PEGs and the large synergistic company. Clearly, the contenders knew that their current proposals would need to be significantly enhanced if they wanted to stay in the running to purchase the company.

The M&A advisor's analysis proved to be very persuasive. Shortly after the analysis was distributed and a few questions were answered, new offers started coming in from the PEGs and the synergistic company. The new offers represented improvements on the original offers by 25 percent to as much as 100 percent. *Yes, that's right!* One of the contenders actually doubled its initial offer, which was to the tune of an increase of $25 million. The excitement was palpable.

But did the M&A firm stop there? No. The client ultimately accepted an offer for an additional increase of $5 million ($55 million total) from the large synergistic company, representing a value more than four times the client's initial value estimate.

How did this happen? During the period after the initial proposals to purchase the company were received, but before the client was locked into a no-shop period, the advisory team reached out to one of the company's primary competitors to determine whether it might have an interest in acquiring the business. This particular competitor was targeted because it was owned by a large multibillion-dollar revenue company, and was known to be suffering from some operational difficulties.

Furthermore, the parent company was on a mission to acquire competitors, evidenced by the fact that it already had completed numerous acquisitions in other industries throughout the current year and in the past few years. The team shared some limited financial information with the competitor, and a few cursory discussions occurred.

However, before any meaningful dialogue could be established, the client had to act on the synergistic company's current offer, which included a no-shop period. The synergistic company's offer was too good not to accept; thus, dialogue with the competitor was terminated. Would the client and his advisors be left wondering forever what might have been with the competitor if only the process could have evolved further down the path? Well, the simple answer is no.

The competitor refused to be deterred by the fact that neither the seller nor anyone on his team could discuss a transaction. Apparently, the competitor was very enthused about the potential of acquiring the client's company, and the lack of a dialogue or information exchange was not going to stand in the way.

This became evident when a purchase proposal showed up from the competitor, even though the no-shop provision was in effect. The competitor's initial purchase proposal represented a five million dollar increase over the synergistic company's offer, which had already been accepted. Fortunately, the no-shop provision in the accepted offer was based only on elapsed time on the calendar. As such, the ability to open a new dialogue with the industry competitor was only a few weeks away, and everyone determined that this was the right course of action, once the legal commitment to the synergistic company was satisfied.

After anxiously sitting out the waiting period for the no-shop provision to expire, the M&A advisor promptly worked through a new letter of intent. From there, things progressed quite quickly to a completed transaction. The owner, together with his advisors, was confident that the competitor was the best fit to purchase the company and lead it into the future.

As it turned out, the owner stayed on board with the competitor to lead not only his own company but also the competitor's own branded business in the same space.

This is a transaction where both sides were happy with the outcome. The owner got what he wanted: a transaction at top value and much-needed working capital for organic growth. The purchaser also got what it wanted: elimination of a competitor, market share, and knowledge capital to lead it into the future.

Commenting on the M&A advisor, the owner/seller said: "Thank you for all your hard work and good counsel this past year. This deal could not have happened without your keen ability to detect and project the hidden value in our business."

His attorney added: "I have been impressed by your energy and creativity and by your attention to the details, great and small, that can make or break a deal."

Lessons Learned

Several lessons can be learned from this case study, including the following:

▶ **Don't go it alone.** The owner worked closely with his team, led by his financial advisor and Equity Strategies Group (ESG), to determine his one way out. ESG brought in one of its highly qualified M&A firms to do the deal. As identified in this case study, the final purchase price ended up close to $70 million, whereas the highest financial buyer's offer was around $40 million. The seller would have initially been satisfied with $20 million, so you can imagine his appreciation. The cost of an experienced and capable M&A advisor will generally be more than offset by better deal terms—a sales price that will be obtained thanks to the M&A advisor's experience, efforts, and contribution.

▶ **It is important to define and control the sale process.** In the above example, potential buyers and offers were already in hand when the competitor was contacted. This created a competitive landscape and may have helped in obtaining a better offer than would have been made in the absence of such competition.

▶ **Keep an open mind about potential transaction types that might meet your goals and objectives.** In this example, the owner initially was interested in obtaining working capital. The M&A advisor was able to demonstrate that an outright sale might also meet the client's goals and objectives, so both avenues were pursued.

▶ **Don't underestimate the importance of timing.** The owner was trying to fulfill his own need for working capital but was also counseled by the M&A advisor to consider what was happening in the market space, as well as with some competitors. By considering a broader spectrum of items and issues beyond his own immediate need, he realized that the timing was great for an outright sale.

YOUR SELLING STRATEGY

A business owner is faced with a multitude of decisions when considering selling his or her company. These decisions can be overwhelming. Timing is always an important factor.

As illustrated in the case study, as part of the One Way Out process, ESG's goal is to make sure that you navigate the business sales terrain successfully by helping you understand your exit options, preparing you for the exit planning process. We have partnered with a select group of investment banking and merger & acquisitions firms who specialize in selling privately held businesses, as well as professionals who can help implement management buyouts and employee stock ownership plans. This extended team will contribute up front in the exit planning phase and will work in concert with you and your legal, accounting, and financial advisors throughout the process.

Have you ever received an offer to sell your business? What happened? Was it in writing? Why didn't you accept the offer?

The good news for you, as an owner considering selling your business to an outside party, is that the current M&A environment remains strong. Consider these key factors:

Improved Performance and Earnings

- ◗ Most businesses are several years removed from their weakest performing months of the recent recession.
- ◗ Quality companies have shown consecutive quarters of solid earnings growth, which provides confidence.
- ◗ Stronger companies are rapidly separating from average and weak competitors

Strong Corporate Balance Sheets

- ◗ Buyers are ready to write checks.
- ◗ US companies have been stockpiling cash at record levels.
- ◗ Debt levels have paid down significantly over the past several years.

Favorable Credit Markets

▶ Borrowing cost remains at historically low levels for investment-grade companies

▶ Senior lenders have begun to loosen their credit parameters and are lending at higher debt to earnings levels.

Private Equity Cash

▶ Private equity buyout funds have over $535 billion in investable capital.

▶ With fewer deals executed over the past three years and a typical investment holding period of five years, private equity groups are highly incentivized to complete transactions.

▶ Aggressive private equity participation often spurs strategic buyers to increase their bids.

Once you have decided to sell your business, your journey could take as little as a few months or up to one year or more. As with any journey, the more realistic your expectations are, the more likely you are to be pleased with the outcome. In light of that, make your first course of action one of gaining clarity with regard to the value and marketability of your business.

THE MARKETABILITY ASSESSMENT

As you embark on the path to sell your business to an outside party, you need a marketability assessment. This provides a critical foundation for you and your advisors to determine whether you and your business are ready to sell and what the potential range of values might be, and to evaluate possible M&A and investment banking partners who could help you execute your exit. It is the first critical step you will take to learn how to maximize the value of your business.

A marketability assessment is forward looking and endeavors to estimate what an actual buyer would pay for your company based on a combination of past, current, and future performance. It utilizes various databases to examine prevailing EBITDA multiples and other valuation methods applicable to your business and industry. It also studies comparable sales of similar companies by researching recent similar transactions, where data is available.

A well-prepared marketability assessment will bring clarity in the following areas:

▶ An understanding of the value of your business if you were to sell it to a qualified buyer today. A tight range of values is calculated using capitalization of earnings, discounted cash flow, and other methods. (Note that this differs from a historical appraisal prepared for gift or estate tax purposes based on Revenue Ruling 59-60 and similar methods. Those appraisals look backward.)

▶ Recommendations to enhance value based on an assessment of your company's value drivers and potential value detractors.

▶ An overview of the current M&A environment and appetite for potential buyers of your business.

▶ Information regarding the length of time necessary to consummate a sale, and explanation of the steps involved.

▶ An understanding of the fees earned by M&A firms and investment bankers to help you achieve your exit goals.

The marketability assessment process also helps select the "best-fit" M&A or investment banking firm to represent you and your business, based on the criteria described earlier and specific factors, such as its industry expertise, its track record of closing transactions, a proper match of transaction size and type, consideration of the chemistry of the players involved, as well as geographic considerations, such as the company's local, national, and international reach.

After gaining clarity, choosing the "best fit" firm to represent you and your company to the marketplace is the next step to be taken.

FINDING THE RIGHT INVESTMENT BANKER

Choosing the transaction intermediary to help you decide if and when to sell your company—whether that is an investment banker or M&A advisor—is both a subjective and an objective decision. As with any industry, you will find both quality firms and those that are inferior. It is critical that you and your advisors carefully vet the firm you choose to lead you on the journey to sell your business. Does the firm you are considering have knowledge of and experience in buying and selling businesses in your industry? The question is not which type of firm is better but which one is best suited for your specific transaction. You need to "click" with that advisor because together you will be making some of the most critical decisions of your life. It is important that you trust each other.

Objectively, you want someone who understands your industry and has deep and current experience selling entrepreneur-owned middle-market companies like yours.

In addition to probing experience, owners need to assess the transaction intermediaries' people skills. Specifically, carefully consider whether he or she possesses these qualities:

- Strong interpersonal communications skills.

- A deep understanding of what motivates people.

- The ability to predict behavior and adapt to different people, situations, and levels of intensity.

- Superior sales skills.

- The ability to tell the story of your company in a compelling way.

- Interest in your company's competitive advantages. Does he or she have ideas about how to leverage it?

- The skills to formulate creative marketing strategies.

- Sensitivity to your need for confidentiality and commitment to protecting it.

- Good listening skills.

- The ability to provide examples of how he or she has anticipated (and dealt with) challenges in the past.

One quality that is a little more difficult to assess is the investment banker's ability to separate unimportant issues from deal breakers, and to distinguish between a bluff and a deal-ending condition. You also want someone who can separate serious from halfhearted buyers. If your candidate cannot accurately make these judgment calls, it is likely that deal momentum will suffer and your deal will collapse before closing.

Types of Transaction Intermediaries

Intermediaries specializing in business sales take many different forms but generally fall into three broad classes of professional advisors. There are 1) business brokers, 2) middle-market mergers & acquisitions (M&A) advisors, and 3) large-transaction investment bankers. Certainly, the three classes may overlap, but firms tend to fall into one of these three groups.

The primary differences among the groups are based on *deal size, methodology, type of buyer,* and *compensation.*

Deal size refers to the value of the transaction. Business brokers typically focus on transactions valued up to $10 million. Middle-market M&A firms generally focus on deals valued from $10 million to $150 million, while large-transaction investment banking firms typically handle transactions valued at more than $150 million.

Methodology relates to the process and systems employed by the intermediary. Business brokers work with a process similar to real estate sales. They focus on acquiring a large inventory of listings and rely on business opportunity advertising. Additionally, business brokers tend to focus on local and community-based businesses, such as restaurants, dry cleaners, pet stores, auto body shops, lawn care companies, and convenience stores. Relative to the other segments, they spend little time on presale planning, tax planning, and packaging. Their informal marketing style is composed primarily of local mass advertising and contacts within their personal networks.

The *middle-market* M&A firms are characterized by heavy presale and tax planning, deep research, and wide marketing outreach. They spend significant time on the front end while developing a comprehensive deal book that outlines and discusses all of the key components of the business. Their methodology is heavily focused on researching the marketplace to identify strategic and private equity buyers, and executing a comprehensive marketing campaign to attract their interest. They will employ either a "negotiated sale" process where they target only a few potential buyers, or a full-blown competitive auction process to attract multiple offers that they can leverage. This process can be scaled down or ramped up, depending on the seller's objectives.

Large-transaction firms, investment bankers, tend to employ a financial engineering methodology. They spend the greatest amount of time on presale planning and financial analysis. The universe of purchasers for large companies is much smaller, so less time is spent on actual marketing. Frequently, the ability to create financial synergy is the motivating factor behind large deals.

The *type of buyer* involved in a business broker's transaction is typically an individual characterized by the following: he or she is usually looking to buy a job, has minimal cash flow, is reliant on seller financing, and has little or no experience as a business owner. With middle-market M&A and large-transaction investment banking firms, buyers tend to be larger privately owned companies, private equity firms, family offices, or public companies. They normally have plenty of cash available for transactions or have bank financing in place, as well as experience in business acquisitions.

The *compensation* structure for a business broker is usually 10 percent to 12 percent of the transaction, paid at closing. Middle-market M&A and investment banking firms are typically paid in the form of a commitment fee, or retainer, paid in advance (or over several months), sometimes credited against a performance fee paid upon closing. Commitment fees typically range from $35,000 to $60,000 for middle-market companies. Performance or success fees frequently have a tiered structure starting in the 4 percent to 6 percent range, depending on the company size, and often have additional performance bonuses based on achieving superior results.

TYPES OF BUYERS

The types of buyers interested in buying your business can be categorized as:

Strategic Buyer

A strategic buyer would be one in the same industry as yours, or closely related. A strategic buyer may even be a competitor. Characteristics of strategic buyers include:

- Strategic buyers have similar customers/process (manufacturing, distribution, services, etc.).
- Potential exists for extensions of existing product or service lines (horizontal).
- Vertical integration can be achieved by purchasing vendors or customers.
- Geographical expansion is often their goal.
- Strategic buyers typically want to buy 100 percent of a business.

Strategic buyers are looking for potential synergies, such as the following:

- Cost synergies: These include the ability to leverage existing infrastructure to reduce costs, better purchasing of raw materials and other inputs, and sales synergies.
- Selling more product or services to existing customers of buyer or seller.
- Introduction of new customers to buyer.
- Elimination of a competitor.

Strategic buyers are sometimes willing to pay a premium price for achieving their synergies. A savvy M&A advisor can exploit the synergistic reasons a strategic buyer wants to buy your business and negotiate a price in excess of typical valuation expectations.

Private Equity

These are also called financial buyers, and they are private equity groups (PEGs), funds, and firms. They look for platform companies that hold a solid niche in their desired markets. They invest in businesses

Beauty is in the eye of the buyer.

and often allow previous owners to retain some "upside" in a transaction and have a longer transition with a qualified partner by acquiring a portion (either minority or majority recapitalization) of a business. Private equity buyers tend to focus on their rate of return and typically hold for three to five years, add value, and then sell. If an owner is ready to sell all or a portion now, but is open to staying with the company for a period of time, selling to a PEG can be advantageous.

Family Office

This is a private equity type of buyer that usually does not have a short "hold period" and can own the business for many years. Family offices view the purchase of a business as a long-term investment.

USING RECAPITALIZATION

Do you want to sell 100 percent of your company or just a portion of it? A recapitalization, or recap, allows you to take some "chips off the table" and sell a portion of your business to a private equity buyer.

Recapitalizations are generally appropriate for owners who:

- want to stay active and retain ownership in their companies;
- are able to work for someone else; and
- can tolerate the risk that a marriage with a PEG may not be made in heaven.

Benefits of a recapitalization include the following:

- Allows owners to convert a portion of their business to cash. PEGs prefer a majority position—70 percent to 80 percent—but some PEGs may take a minority position if the seller is an outstanding operator.

- Reduces owner's risk through asset diversification and transfer of personal guarantees to the PEG.

- May allow the owner to remain in charge of the company, typically for two to three years. On occasion, PEGs require the owner to remain with the company and the term is negotiable.

- Injects into the company the cash necessary to expand, hire new employees, and/or fund additional acquisitions.

- Increases the yield on owner's remaining interest in the company if PEG ownership is successful.

- Rewards key managers, as the PEG usually creates option plans that give key managers a piece of future growth of the company.

If you think recapitalization meets your exit goals, consider the following:

- How you might retain control via real estate leases (leasing the business real estate to the PEG gives the seller some leverage).

- How the seller might retain control via different classes of stock (sales can be structured so that one class of stock owns the profits while another class retains control).

- Whether you can afford to lose your investment (retained interest) if the arrangement with the PEG does not go well.

Knowledge is power when an owner decides to sell a business. For most owners, the business sale process is a mountain of uncertainty. Surrounding yourself with the right advisors is critical to finding the right buyer, finding the right transaction, and maximizing the selling price of your company.

THE SALES PROCESS

With ESG, you and your investment banker will develop a plan for the actual sale of the business, including such items as defining your business's value and determining how to handle offers. At the appropriate time, you will release information, on a confidential basis, about your company to generate buyers' interest. Once you have decided on a buyer, your team will help negotiate the terms and conditions of the sale. Finally, you will work with your investment banker, attorney, and CPA to complete due diligence and close the deal.

The following steps illustrate the typical flow of a deal from beginning to end:

▶ **Step 1:** Financial review of the company to determine valuation ranges and marketability (i.e., prepare marketability assessment).

▶ **Step 2:** Creation and sharing of results from marketability assessment. If objectives, valuation expectations, and timing are in alignment, proceed to step 3. If not, continue to work on business until ready.

▶ **Step 3:** Initial meeting with M&A advisor.

▶ **Step 4:** Retain M&A advisor and prepare to go to market.

▶ **Step 5:** Deal marketing to attract buyers.

▶ **Step 6:** Negotiation and execution of letter of intent.

▶ **Step 7:** Due diligence.

▶ **Step 8:** Closing.

Steps 1, 2, and 3 are conducted to understand your objectives, review financial statements (balance sheets and P&L statements for several years), and interview you to gain understanding of your business model and value expectations to determine the probability of success before an agreement to work together is established. Step 4 is the finalization of the engagement agreement between the M&A advisor and the seller. The core process of selling a company begins with step 5, deal marketing, and concludes with step 8, closing.

SELLING A BUSINESS REQUIRES A TREMENDOUS AMOUNT OF DEAL MARKETING WHILE UTILIZING MANY DIFFERENT AVENUES, INCLUDING INDUSTRY CONTACTS, DATABASES, AND ACCESS TO PRIVATE EQUITY.

Step 6, negotiating, requires management of all the relationships in a transaction with a keen understanding of each party's goals and objectives. Success in this step, just as in every other step of selling a business, requires a specific, proven process that will steer away from potential pitfalls, instead utilizing negotiations and leverage to maximize the number of offers received, highest values, and best terms.

The final step is closing the deal. Frequently the most difficult step in the entire process is moving all of the interested parties to a successful closing. Even in the best of circumstances, this is a complicated process.

Creating Multiple Options

Creating multiple options relates to the ability to gather and manage several buyers at the same time. The most common mistake a business owner makes when selling a business is dealing with only one interested party at a time. This limits not only an owner's likelihood of landing a successful deal but also the number of potential offers. Momentum is important, and speed to closing creates urgency. M&A advisors are experts at creating and maintaining positive momentum and the right environment to close.

Process Types

There are three types of M&A or investment banking processes that can be utilized:

- **Pre-emptive buyer:** Approaching one or a few buyers before embarking on a competitive auction process. This will "test the market" and often leads to a more robust auction.

- **Targeted auction:** Approaching a limited number of buyers competing against each other.

- **Competitive auction:** This is an exhaustive search for multiple financial and strategic buyers to achieve the best value and terms for the seller, as shown in Figure 4.1.

If the competitive auction process is managed effectively, it leads to a greater probability of securing several interested parties. It is important to maintain confidentiality through this process, and M&A firms know to do this. Garnering multiple interested parties provides much greater clarity in evaluating the merits of each offer, and it increases the likelihood that a stronger value with better times will be received by the seller.

Potential benefits of the competitive auction process include the following:

- It increases likelihood of finding the best buyer for your business at the highest price and best terms.

- It minimizes time disruption to seller and enables seller to continue running the business.

Figure 4.1. Here's an example of steps involved in the competitive auction process.

- ▶ It forces a timely closing by holding buyers to a predetermined time schedule.

- ▶ It enables owner to assess the potential buyers' intentions for the business after closing through interviews.

- ▶ It empowers a third party, the M&A firm, to negotiate/advocate for the seller with limited emotion.

- ▶ It brings multiple opportunities to negotiate price and terms. As the old saying goes, "One buyer is *no* buyer." Negotiating leverage is likely to yield the highest price and best terms.

Stay Focused on Your Business

The biggest risk a business owner faces when attempting to exit is the inability to stay focused on managing the core business. Without an M&A advisor managing the selling process, the owner may become distracted in two ways: time and mental energy. An owner might wake up one day to find that he is spending a majority of his or her time on the transaction instead of his or her customers, employees, and day-to-day activities that keep the business running smoothly.

Obviously, the best time to sell a business is when performance is at a peak or is showing signs of continued growth. This gives the company maximum bragging rights, as it touts such effective practices as an efficient team, a large and satisfied customer base, increasing profits, quality products, excellent goodwill, and other attributes associated with a successful business. Not surprisingly, buyers willingly pay top dollar to acquire such a business.

Selling a business that is performing well is of mutual benefit to both the seller and the buyer. While the seller realizes a premium price, promising a secure future, the buyer acquires a well-organized addition to the existing core competencies of the acquiring business. With minimal adjustments, the buyer can hopefully expand his or her reach with the newly acquired business.

Presale Planning

A well-prepared, carefully executed sale of a business process can take anywhere from six months to a year—or even more once you begin.

Before you embark on the selling process, you should engage in presale planning. This is, of course, part of the overall One Way Out process. Presale planning has two components:

◗ Personal planning

◗ Business planning

Personal presale planning requires you to meet with a qualified, experienced financial advisor who can gauge your mental and financial readiness and calculate what you will need to net from a sale to attain your vision of financial independence. Consider all sources of income you will have after the sale, as well as future living expenses. Don't forget to build in taxes, inflation, different rates of return, cost of long-term care, and so on.

Calculate several different scenarios to "stress test" your model to make sure you will be financially secure before you leap. This process allows you to clearly define your options and implement strategies that will enable you to exit your business on your own terms and at the most appropriate time. Minimizing income taxes upon sale is the number one issue for most owners. Strategic presale planning can help reduce the IRS's cut. A plan to invest business sale proceeds should be developed prior to closing the transaction.

As discussed in chapter 7, your wealth preservation plan should be updated and enhanced through proactive planning, as well. For example, you may want to transfer part of your company to your children, or a trust for their benefit, prior to selling so that the gifted portion will be outside of your taxable estate. You may also consider the use of charitable giving strategies to minimize income and estate tax consequences.

A major goal in each transaction is to maximize the value of the business and create liquidity for the owner, whether a stock or asset sale, a merger, a partial sale, or recapitalization.

Business presale planning involves preparing your business for the selling process. Take stock of value drivers and value detractors. Many of these will surface during the marketability assessment phase, so get started.

Value Drivers

What is a value driver? It is a factor that increases the value and marketability of a business.

Some value drivers are external, while others are internal. External factors such as extent of competition (both foreign and

Prepare your business by paying attention to the value drivers. The worst-case scenario is you'll end up with a well-run company.

domestic), barriers to entry, economic trends, market size, and industry growth are variables that are beyond your control.

The factors you can control—ones that influence the appeal of your business—are internal to your company. Have you ever wondered why some companies command a premium valuation at the top of the multiple range, while others fall well below the median? They pay attention to value drivers.

AS A BUSINESS OWNER, YOUR ABILITY TO POSITIVELY INFLUENCE THE INTERNAL VALUE DRIVERS WILL DIRECTLY IMPACT THE VALUE OF YOUR COMPANY WHEN IT IS TIME TO EXIT.

It is wise to work on internal value drivers to build the best possible business you can so that you are always ready to sell your company when the time is right. The following provides an overview of 12 value drivers that require your attention as you strive to maximize the marketability and value of your business.

1. Sales Trends

We all know that the main objective of a company is to generate an acceptable return to its shareholders. Not surprisingly, then, a business with steady annual increases in sales is considered more valuable than others. How would you describe your current sales trends? Increasing, flat, or decreasing? Volatile? What about your industry and the market for your products and services?

2. Profit Trends

As a business owner, you already know that generating a profit is the final imperative for your firm's success. Breaking even leaves you with insufficient funds to meet unexpected expenditures or invest in expansion plans. Real growth requires profit. The ability to buy assets and new machinery, employ more people, invest in research and development and training, and explore new markets takes capital.

If your company does not generate significant profits, the chance of receiving top dollar for it is greatly minimized. Identify the factors causing a negative impact on your profits. As a business owner, you must be in touch with everything that happens in your company. Consider these questions:

▶ How would you describe or calculate profitability over the past three years? What are your projections for this year and beyond?

▶ How do your margins compare to your industry?

3. Recurring Revenue

The Holy Grail for many buyers is a recurring revenue stream. Better still when that recurring revenue is contractual. Which statement best describes your company's recurring revenue: once a sale is made, is it rare to sell again to that same customer, or do most customers place recurring orders? To maximize value, take a critical look at your customer base and, whenever possible, develop a recurring revenue stream.

4. Unique Selling Proposition

What's unique about the products and services offered by your company? Consumers know the products they prefer, even when they may not be familiar with the actual company. Customers typically opt for goods with unique features, frequently referred to as the unique selling proposition (USP).

Are your products unique and clearly differentiated with a brand identity? If so, are they protected by trademarks, patents, or copyrights? What percentage of annual revenues stem from your unique products or services?

5. Customer Concentration

Customer concentration refers to the degree to which a company has a substantial percentage of revenues generated by a small group of customers. High customer concentration points to a handful of customers contributing significantly to the total annual revenues of a company. Buyers want a broad, diverse customer base. Preferably, there is a reliable stream of recurring revenue, and transferable contracts are in place.

Generally, if one customer represents 20 percent or more of your business, you are approaching the "danger zone." The obvious disadvantage of this situation is the risk of incurring huge losses with the departure of any one of your top customers. In addition, these few customers tend to exert greater leverage against the business. Consider the following:

▶ Do you have a few customers that make up the majority of sales?

‣ If so, what is your plan to diversify?

‣ Are customer relationships long-standing and repetitive?

‣ Are your customer relationships and/or contracts transferable?

6. Sales and Marketing

A strong sales and marketing program is the driving force behind a successful company. With the advent of social media, the marketing landscape is evolving rapidly.

‣ Does your marketing plan include tried and tested strategies that have worked for your company over the years as well as new initiatives designed to attract new customers?

‣ Are your overall sales and marketing processes and plans well documented and consistently executed?

‣ Market share: what percentage of the market do you have?

7. Vendor Reliance

Good business practice dictates that you should have a diverse number of vendors or suppliers to protect yourself in the event that one of them experiences problems. Changes in business practices and outsourcing have increased the degree of vendor reliance. Consider these questions:

‣ Are you dependent on any one or two key vendors?

‣ How will you manage if one of your key vendors goes out of business tomorrow or is unable to meet your needs?

‣ Do you have viable alternatives available?

8. Key Employees

As a business owner, you already know that running a business alone is impossible; you need a strong team of employees. Usually a handful are truly key to the success of the business. Recruiting, retaining, and rewarding that team is critical for an organization to be successful over the long term. The quality of your management team can have a significant impact on the value of your business. Consider these questions:

‣ Is your business very dependent on you to continue to run it successfully?

‣ Who are your key people? How would the business suffer if they left?

▶ Do you have non-solicitation or non-compete agreements?

▶ What programs do you have in place to retain and incentivize key employees to achieve your goals for the company?

- Nonqualified deferred compensation plans
- Golden handcuffs/vesting schedules
- Synthetic equity
- Split dollar insurance
- Other perks

9. Competition

A clear competitive advantage makes your business more valuable. Why do your customers do business with you over your competitors? What separates you from your competitors? Consider the basis on which you compete favorably—is it price, service, selection, or location? Why are you the provider of choice for your customers?

10. Transferability

How easy would it be for a new owner to step into your company and maintain the relationships you have built over the years? Evaluate your company on its ability to hold customer, vendor, and employee relationships in place if it were sold.

11. Barriers to Entry

Some businesses required a high level of capital investment, technical expertise, and other specific qualifications, while others are easy to start up. How high are the barriers to entry in your industry? Can anyone get into it or just a select few? What keeps them out? A prospective buyer often needs to decide whether to start up a business or buy yours—why is it easier or beneficial to buy your business? How much do outside influences affect your company's ability to grow?

12. Technology or Process Advantages

Highly valuable businesses have specific technological or proprietary process advantages over the rest of their industry. Which does your company possess? It is far ahead of the industry or lagging? Is your business model highly automated?

You will find more information on building your business's value in chapter 5, "Growing Your Business along the Value Path."

YOUR VALUE DRIVER ASSESSMENT

We have compiled an assessment tool to address these 12 value drivers with a rating system that will help to determine your company's strengths and weaknesses. In preparing to sell your company, you must carefully consider these value drivers. Of course, there are many other factors and nuances that you also must take into account, but this is a good start.

An optimal approach would be for you to rate your company, and then have your financial advisor or an investment banker rate it, as well. Sometimes your perception is skewed on the basis of your perception of areas that you are directly involved with and the risk you associate with each one.

Why do some companies sell for more than others in the same industry? Value drivers.

A value driver measures systems, processes, and resources that create sustainable value. Rate your company for each of the twelve value drivers shown in Figure 4.2 by placing an "X" in the box that is most reflective. Use 1 for the lowest score and 5 for the highest. Clearly more 5s are desirable.

Value Drivers	1 (low)	2	3	4	5 (high)
1. Positive Sales Trends					
2. Positive Profit Trends					
3. High Recurring Revenue					
4. Unique Selling Proposition					
5. Low Customer Concentration					
6. Strong Sales & Marketing					
7. Low Vendor Reliance					
8. Strong Key Employees					
9. Low Competition					
10 Easy to Transfer					
11. High Barriers to Entry					
12. Technology/Process Advantages					

Figure 4.2. Your Value Driver Assessment can help you obtain top value for your business. To complete the full assessment, go to www.equitystrategiesgroup.com.

The goal is to get a picture of where your strengths and areas for improvement are. Please take a few moments and complete the Value Driver Assessment for your company on the previous page.

Value Detractors

A value detractor is the absence or underdevelopment of a value driver. Several examples are listed here:

- Company is stagnant or shrinking in revenues and profits.
- Poor or incomplete financial systems and accounting records.
- Undocumented systems/processes.
- Industry outlook is bleak.
- Emergence of significant competition.
- Customer/vendor concentration issues.
- Inability to retain key employees/high turnover.
- Management team ready for retirement, en masse.

Here's a very important point: your company will never be perfect. That's okay, because buyers enjoy seeing the opportunity for improvement in their purchase; it offers them a chance to bring additional value post-transaction. However, some detractors can adversely affect the top valuation you seek when making a sale. Some may go so far as to be classified as nonstarters or "deal killers." Examples include the following:

- Material environmental issues
- Pending lawsuits
- Known threats to relationships with key employees, vendors, or customers
- Significantly underfunded defined benefit pension plans

If any of these issues impact your company, you should make it a top priority to address them before going to market.

To sum up the importance of value drivers and their impact on the selling price of your business, consider the following: a potential buyer will pay more than just some range of industry-accepted multiples of earnings (EBITDA) for it. You will walk away with (hopefully) a premium price based on a high multiple of earnings, plus "excess" cash (in excess of necessary working capital

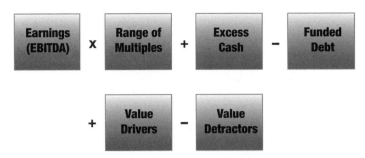

Figure 4.3. Summary of the impact of value drivers and value detractors on selling price.

to run the company) minus outstanding debt that you will repay to lenders, plus value attributable to value drivers you created minus any value detractors:

CONSIDERING YOUR BUSINESS REAL ESTATE

Unless you own a "virtual" company, you operate in a physical facility. Some businesses operate from a single location; others have multiple locations across the United States or the entire world. Consider these questions:

- Is the real estate leased? If so, what are the terms? Are leases assignable? How much time is left on the lease?
- If real estate is owned, how?
  - By you personally?
  - By a separate LLC, partnership, or corporation you own wholly or partially?
  - By the operating company itself?
  - Is there a mortgage(s) outstanding? How much? Terms?
  - Tax basis (for capital gains tax)?
  - Will real estate be kept or sold with the business? Are you flexible?

The sale or leasing of the business real estate to a new owner of your business represents another source of wealth or cash flow. If the location or special features of the property are attractive to a new owner, it may be a package deal.

TAX PLANNING FOR YOUR EXIT

You knew this was coming. You can't make sound plans to exit your business without considering the tax consequences and your overall plans for financial independence. As the cautionary tales sprinkled throughout this book reveal, business owners who fail to create and execute a holistic One Way Out plan including their exit strategy are courting trouble.

WITHOUT A COMPREHENSIVE TAX STRATEGY, THE IRS, NOT YOU OR YOUR FAMILY, WILL BE THE ULTIMATE BENEFICIARY OF MUCH OF YOUR HARD WORK.

I haven't met a single business owner who was planning to leave much of his or her life's work to the federal or state government. But that is exactly what will happen without proper tax planning.

Understanding the taxation of a particular exit strategy is crucial. Some key considerations are as follows:

- Asset sale vs. stock sale
- Avoiding double taxation (C Corporations)
- IRC Section 1202 tax-free sales
- Tax-free reorganizations
- Reverse mergers
- Preserving net operating losses
- Personal goodwill vs. corporate goodwill
- Consulting and noncompete agreements
- Use of charitable planning tools, such as remainder and lead trusts and foundations
- Use of tax-deferred like-kind exchanges of real estate under IRC Section 1031

Entity Selection and Taxes

Choosing the best entity form for your business can have a dramatic impact on its eventual sale. The choice between C or S corporation (or other pass-through entity, such as an LLC) becomes critically important. That's because selling your company's assets inside the wrong entity can cost an extra 40 percent of your sale price.

Operating as a C corporation during start-up and growth years allows you to take advantage of lower tax rates. When you sell your corporate assets, however, you will pay taxes at the corporate level and then *again* at the individual level. Consider this example of how this *double tax hit* affected one seller:

After careful analysis, Franklin decided that he needed $15 million from the sale of his business (FRANCO). Given that Franklin had a valuation performed that valued his software design company at about $20 million, Franklin's goal was realistic. He anticipated 25 percent capital gains tax (20 percent federal and 5 percent state) and was ready to sell.

As part of a marketability assessment, ESG and the owner's financial advisor reviewed FRANCO's financial statements, noting that there were not a lot of hard assets (meaning most of the purchase price would be paid for corporate goodwill—an asset without any basis) and that FRANCO was organized as a C corporation. We suggested to Franklin that this entity choice would prove to be a major stumbling block because most buyers would want to buy the assets of FRANCO—not its stock. As a C corporation, his tax bill would be closer to $10 million.

Franklin was shocked as we explained that the IRS would tax FRANCO at the corporate level on the difference between what the corporation paid for the assets and the $20 million sale price of the assets. At most, FRANCO's basis was $5 million, so that tax would be assessed on a gain of $15 million. Because the effective tax rate is approximately 39 percent, the tax paid by FRANCO would approach $6 million. When Franklin then received the remaining $15 million from FRANCO, the IRS would impose a capital gains tax on Franklin's gain. Assuming a 25 percent capital gains rate, Franklin would pay about $3,750,000 because he had very little basis in the stock. The net proceeds to Franklin were not $15 million, but just over $10 million.

If Franklin had operated FRANCO as an S Corp or other "pass-through" tax entity, such as an LLC, the tax result would have been dramatically different.

How can you avoid this tax disaster when you sell your company? Some C corporation owners insist upon a stock-only sale.

This is a great theory, but over 60 percent of all M&A transactions in the last several years were asset sales. Restricting your pool of buyers to those willing to purchase only stock significantly limits the number of possible candidates.

Converting your company from a C corporation to an S corporation is an option, but five years must then pass before the tax law allows full S corporation tax treatment. If you don't have five years left in you, converting now to an S corporation may still offer some tax benefits. The sooner you convert to an S corporation, the greater the likelihood of tax savings.

Other Tax Reduction Strategies

Other strategies to minimize taxation on the sale of assets with a C corporation include the following:

- Sale of "personal" goodwill outside of the C corporation
- Noncompete and consulting agreements
- Contribution and sale agreements, if there will be equity owned after the transaction
- Code section 338h(10) election
- Charitable remainder trusts

Other tax planning techniques fall into three categories: deduct (generating tax deductions), divert (to a different, lower tax bracket), and defer (postpone payment of taxes into the future).

Deduct

- Charitable gifts
- Contributions to a qualified retirement plan, such as 401(k), profit-sharing plan, defined benefit pension, or SEP pre- or post-sale if self-employed.
- ESOP contributions
- Oil and gas and other partnerships

▶ Pay family director's fees

▶ Real estate loss deduction, matched with passive income generators

▶ Long-term care insurance deduction (C corp)

Divert

▶ Income to children and other lower tax brackets

▶ Gifts of business interests to children to transfer income to lower tax brackets

▶ Family on payroll

▶ Life insurance as supplemental retirement income, tax-free withdrawals/ loans

Defer

▶ Deferred payments in connection with sale of business

▶ Earn-outs

▶ Self-financed sale arrangements

▶ Roth IRA conversion

▶ Sale to ESOP utilizing code section 1042 to postpone gain on sale (C corp)

▶ Nonqualified deferred compensation

▶ Code section 1031 and 1035 to defer taxation of gain on real estate, annuities, or life insurance.

▶ 401(k), profit sharing plans, and other qualified retirement plans

▶ Split dollar compensation arrangements

▶ Life insurance for qualified plan conversion to Roth IRA at death for heirs

YOUR FINANCIAL TAKEAWAY

The art of exit planning includes structuring an exit strategy that meets your objectives and maximizes after-tax proceeds. So how much will you take with you after all is said and done? Figure 4.4 illustrates one calculation.

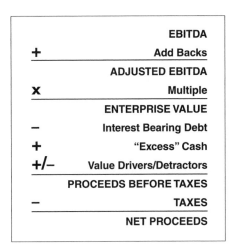

Figure 4.4 How much will you walk away with? This calculation will help you determine the number.

AFTER THE CLOSE

So what happens after your successful exit? Based on feedback from our clients, you can expect more golf, travel with your family, perhaps writing a book, starting another business, building a home shop to play in, more time with classic cars or horses, more time on the boat, and even learning to fly a plane. Whatever your vision, your ideal future can be yours.

CHAPTER SUMMARY

Selling your business to an outside buyer is the preferred exit strategy to maximize the value you receive, create liquidity, and sever risk. However, you should not try to sell your business on your own, since it is a complex process fraught with land mines. You therefore should execute this critical process with the assistance of a professional transaction intermediary—either a mergers and acquisitions (M&A) advisor or an investment banker—who can focus 100 percent on selling businesses like yours for maximum value.

Be sure to have a strategy in place. Well in advance of your sale—even years ahead—make sure that your business is structured in a way that minimizes your tax burden. Without a comprehensive tax strategy, the IRS, rather than you or your family, will be the ultimate beneficiary of much of your hard work.

Conduct a marketability assessment. This provides a critical foundation for you and your advisors to determine whether you and your business are ready to sell, and what the potential range of values might be and allows you to evaluate possible M&A and investment banking partners who could help you execute your exit. It is the first critical step you will take to learn how to maximize the value of your business.

Pay attention to your business's *value drivers* in order to garner the maximum selling price. External factors such as extent of competition (both foreign and domestic), barriers to entry, economic trends, market size, and industry growth are variables that are beyond your control. However, you can control interval value drivers such as sales and profit trends, recurring revenue, your unique selling proposition, customer concentration, key employees, and other important factors.

Once you begin the selling process, take the time with your intermediary to fully discuss and understand your potential buyers, whether they are *strategic buyers* looking to create synergies or eliminate competition with a business they already have, or *private equity buyers*, who tend to focus on an anticipated rate of return over limited or longer terms.

Let your sales intermediary take your company through the process, creating sales options and managing multiple process types, while you continue to focus on running your business every day.

In the end, following this One Way Out process for sale to an outside party will give you the best opportunity to realize your dreams and move on to the next phase of your life with financial security. And remember that there *is* a definite process to follow. Don't go at it alone. Selling your business is not a do-it-yourself proposition, for a variety of reasons. A team of professionals, including your Business Intelligence Specialist, M&A advisor, financial advisor, CPA, and attorney, will provide expertise toward a successful outcome.

PART TWO

SUPPORTING YOUR EXIT STRATEGY

Chapter 5

Growing Your Business along the Value Path

THE *VALUE PATH* SUMMARIZES the life cycle of a typical business. Entrepreneurs often spend the better part of their adult lives nurturing and growing a business. They take on significant risk because they are passionate about their ability to compete in the marketplace and win on the basis of their ideas, products, and services. Their companies survive, thrive, and ideally pass along their value path through the *early stage* and the *growth stage*, to the *late stage,* and then on to the owners' point of exit.

The majority of business owners are in the growth stage. You probably are, too. During this critical period, it is important that you address the key factors that are necessary to continue your upward track—especially if you're planning for your optimal exit someday. This chapter looks at the things you should do to foster your growth stage on the value path.

CASE STUDY:
PLANNING FOR THE CLOSELY HELD/FAMILY BUSINESS

This real-world case study illustrates some likely needs and planning opportunities a business can face along its value path. It looks at a family-owned business and the owner's objective to grow the business, protect assets, and keep the business in the family for future generations.

Company History

This company, named The Greatest Generation, or simply TGG, was started in 1945 in Brooklyn, New York. The Dodgers were still at Ebbets Field. Like most New Yorkers, the family who started this small business worshiped their beloved "Brooklyn Bums." "Dem Bums" helped cheer up a woman, Blanche, who became a widow at an unfair young age with two children to feed. She and her two boys, Gene and Robert, had hatched an idea to find used equipment, recondition it, and sell it. Over the years, the company grew exponentially and moved during 1964, in need of more space. The owners bought several acres of land and built a 160,000-square-foot manufacturing plant somewhere in the swamps of Jersey, years before the region became heavily industrialized.

In 1975, the matriarch passed away and left TGG to her two sons. At that time, gross sales had just topped $1 million. The sons hired aggressively and grew the business from 3 employees to, ultimately, 350. Since 1979, they have run three shifts per day. Gross sales today are in excess of $100 million per year.

Family History

Son Gene has two children, Henry and Jody, who left the business when their father was bought out. Robert has three sons, Herb, Lenny, and Ken. The first son, Herb, came into the business for a brief period of time and realized it wasn't a good fit. He ultimately left the business and the country. The second son, Lenny, graduated from college under a work-study program and worked for several years for a large public company to get his feet wet and learn about the business world on a bigger scale. The understanding was that he would come into the family business, which he did in his mid-twenties. He is excelling and is the driving force behind the business today. The youngest son, Ken, also came into the business after college and is doing quite well.

Gene also had a son, Louis, who is active in the business.

Family Tree

Blanche – Founder
    Gene – Son
        Henry – Grandson
        Jody – Granddaughter
    Robert – Son
        Herb – Grandson
        Lenny – Grandson
            Mike – Great Grandson
            Ellie – Great Granddaughter
        Ken – Grandson
            Natasha – Great Granddaughter

Business Valuation

When I met the owners in 1990, TGG never had undergone a formal business valuation. At the time, annual gross sales were in excess of $22 million. The net profits were several million dollars per year, including owners' compensations. Furthermore, the company had a very strong balance sheet, little bank debt, and a growing, diverse customer base. Conservatively, TGG may have been worth $20 million.

Succession Planning

Robert and Gene had a stock redemption buy/sell agreement with a ridiculously low and outdated value of $500,000 each. A major concern was that if one of them died, the corporation (to the benefit of the surviving brother) could buy the business for a dramatic bargain price. Furthermore, neither family was prepared to pay the enormous estate tax that would result. As the brothers were now well into their seventies, this was becoming an imminent reality. Also, it was becoming evident that the next generation of children lacked the ability to work well together.

All three sons were paid equally, even though Robert's sons, Lenny and Ken, had more responsibility, worked harder, and demonstrated more effectiveness in their current business roles than did Louis. Brothers Robert and Gene disagreed vehemently on compensation issues. Gene thought that all pay should be equal, while Robert believed pay should be based on merit. Finally, this disagreement boiled over, and Gene said, "Buy me out!"

Family Buyout

The objective was to buy out Gene and, at the same time, avoid any increases in Robert's already sizeable taxable estate. The solution was to design a buyout during Gene's lifetime. Rather than having his seventy-two-year-old brother buy him out and inflate his taxable estate, the recommended solution would bypass Robert so that his two sons who were the most active in the business, Lenny and Ken (who were in their midthirties), would buy out their uncle.

A reasonable value was placed on Gene's 50-percent interest in TGG, and he was bought out through a promissory note over ten years at a fixed imputed interest rate. Lenny and Ken used cash flow from the business, as S-corporation dividend distributions, to buy out their uncle (and rid themselves of their cousin) while increasing their ownership percentages and tax bases.

Today Robert and his two sons own 33 percent each. Gene, in turn, received a fair value for his share of the business and a sizable stream of income over the next ten years.

New Buy/Sell Agreement

Creating a buy/sell agreement between grandsons Lenny and Ken was now imperative. So, TGG created a cross-purchase agreement, funded appropriately with life and disability insurance to protect the corporation, the shareholders, and their families.

Key Employees

Lenny and Ken's future success became focused on retaining and rewarding the key people who would help drive further growth. They identified the top eight employees who were the key to the company's future success and growth. While the company paid a fair wage, it needed to design a benefits program to "handcuff" and reward these eight key employees for staying with the company until retirement age, and to provide incentive to reach specified profitability and performance milestones.

We designed a two-step program as follows:

A 401(k)/profit-sharing plan for all full-time employees. During enrollment, employees were educated to fully appreciate the income tax benefits and retirement resources being provided by their employer.

A nonqualified deferred compensation plan to selectively benefit and incentivize the key employees only. This plan provided supplemental retirement income, disability income, and death benefits to their families if they should become disabled or die while employed by the company. It has proven to be highly effective; they have not lost a single employee since adopting it fifteen years ago, while sales, profitability, and business value have increased dramatically.

The Future Is Bright

As competitors continue to go out of business or consolidate, TGG is thriving and expanding. It has made several acquisitions of synergistic businesses and now operates four facilities in addition to the company headquarters and primary manufacturing plant. TGG has a fleet of more than 100 trailers that deliver product all across North America, although the New York/New Jersey metropolitan area still represents the majority of the market served. Recently the company achieved $100 million in gross sales.

Raising Capital

The biggest challenge facing TGG today is that it has outgrown its current facilities, having been on a major growth path, and is in the process of acquiring a new plant. This will stimulate the local economy and create new jobs.

The company qualifies for various tax credits from which tax benefits will be realized over the next ten years. It has partnered with a strategic investor to help finance its expansion plans. A portion of the stock was recently sold to the strategic investor at seven times the adjusted EBITDA (Earnings Before Interest, Taxes, Depreciation, and Amortization) multiple. The owners received cash, retained control, and still own all of the business real estate (which is in a separate legal entity). They have also received additional working capital and salary continuation and have maintained all perks.

The new expansion plans include construction of a 500,000-square-foot facility on ninety-five acres, with enough space to park 450 trailers and access to eight rail cars. They have created more than 200 new jobs. Sales are projected to soar past $100 million.

Conclusion

Here is a review some of the major problems and threats encountered in the TGG case study:

- Lack of proper business valuation to ensure that the first shareholder to die did not lose tremendous value for his family

- Need to buy out the uncle and, ideally, avoid inflation of Robert's taxable estate

- Establishment of a proper buy/sell agreement between grandchildren at a reasonable value and funding it to carry out the terms of the agreement in the event of death or disability

- Reduction of estate taxes and settlement costs to avoid involuntary liquidation of business and real estate to pay the IRS.

- Retention of key employees to provide second-line management strength for continued business success and achievement of future expansion plans.

- Search for growth capital and a strategic partner (this resulted in a partial sale, i.e., an equity recapitalization)

Results

- A formal business valuation of TGG was completed to establish fair-market value for transfer tax purposes and buyouts.

- A nonqualified deferred compensation plan was implemented, including retirement benefits, key person life insurance, and disability insurance for the top eight employees.

- New wills, durable powers of attorney, and living wills were executed for all shareholders. Lenny and Ken's wills recently were updated with provisions to allow business stock to pass to Mike, Ellie, and Natasha (Blanche's great-grandchildren), with detailed language to buy stock back if they choose to leave the business.

- Business real estate was sold to an intentionally defective income trust (IDIT) to reduce estate tax liability on assets passing from Robert to his sons.

- Family Limited Partnership/Grantor Retained Annuity Trusts (FLP/GRATs) were implemented to further reduce estate tax exposure (and transfer 16 percent of Robert's stock to his sons).

- A 401(k) plan was created to provide for retirement savings of owners and all eligible employees.

- Personal life insurance was purchased for family members.

- Investment planning began for future financial independence.

- Equity recapitalization raised much-needed capital for expansion.

THE VALUE PATH PROCESS

As a business owner, your single largest asset is most likely your business. The value path process is focused on maximizing the value of your business and helping you ultimately transfer that value to your balance sheet, family, or charity of choice. A typical business's value path looks like this:

> The value path process is focused on maximizing and transferring the value of your business.

Early Stage

The early stage, a.k.a., "Just Survive," is typically characterized by 24/7 work weeks and a high degree of owner control and autonomy. The owner is often overextended and undercapitalized, while trying to keep creditors at bay, minimize taxes, and reinvest profits to finance future growth, often at personal sacrifice. He or she is renting space, hiring employees, and offering basic fringe benefits, such as medical coverage. Unfortunately, the majority of businesses do not survive the early stage.

Growth Stage

The growth stage, a.k.a., "It's Time to Strive," is characterized by a new feeling of success. The business has made it. Survival is reasonably secure. However, the owner cannot afford to rest on his or her laurels. The challenges of running a growth-stage business include the following:

- Attracting, training, and retaining employees
- Obtaining additional capital, as needed
- Building more infrastructure, inventory, equipment, and real estate
- Staying one step ahead of competitors

Late Stage

During the late stage, a.k.a., "What's Next?" the business owner has become a respected and influential member of the community. He or she now enjoys success and begins to think about how to exit and convert the equity built up inside the business into liquid resources for new opportunities, retirement, transfers to family, or the ability to satisfy charitable intentions.

Throughout these stages, you will be confronted with various concerns and challenges. Every business has them, and regardless of your specifics, you will build maximum value along the way by addressing these basic objectives:

- Saving income taxes
- Creatively attracting, retaining, and rewarding key employees
- Taking advantage of appropriate company fringe benefits
- Achieving ready access to capital
- Protecting your business and other assets from creditors and predators
- Developing an exit strategy so that when you are ready, you can exit your business and obtain maximum dollar value to enjoy your vision of the lifestyle you expect
- Preserving your wealth, allowing you to pass it on to your family

Identifying Your Needs and Challenges

You probably have a pretty good idea already of where your business stands on this value path. However, you'll be able to pinpoint your needs and challenges with respect to finding your One Way Out by assessing the following things:

▶ When did you start your business?

▶ Why did you go into business for yourself?

▶ How did you capitalize it initially and subsequently?

▶ What is your 5/10/20-year plan?

Also consider the following:

▶ What aspects of your business would you like to develop further?

▶ What challenges do you face in taking your business to the next level?

▶ If you could change one aspect of your business, what would it be?

▶ Do you need access to additional capital to grow and expand?

▶ What is your exit strategy?

Now follow the value path diagram, as shown in Figure 5.1, and consider your answers to the questions under each bullet point.

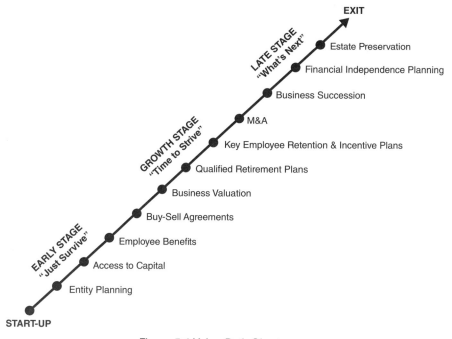

Figure 5.1. Value Path Chart

1. Entity Planning

- Are you structured as a C Corp, S Corp, or LLC?
- Are roles/responsibilities of employees well defined?
- Are systems/processes in place?

2. Access to Capital

- Who is your current bank or other lender?
- What loans/lines of credit are outstanding?
- Are the terms competitive today?
- Do you need more capital?
- How do you plan to take your company to the next level?

3. Employee Benefits

- What fringe benefits does your business provide to you and your employees?
- When were the programs last reviewed?

4. Buy/sell Agreement

- Do you have one?
- What type?
- When was it last reviewed?
- Is it properly funded with life and disability insurance?

5. Business Valuation

- What's it worth?
- How did you arrive at that number? Have you ever had a formal valuation?

6. Qualified Retirement Plans

- What type of plan does your business have in place?
- Are you happy with the investment performance and administration?
- Is it in compliance with latest ERISA and DOL rules?

7. Key Employee Retention & Incentive Plans

- Do you have one?
- Which employees are key to the survival and success of your busi-

ness? What have you done to attract/retain/reward them?

8. Business Succession Planning

- Do you have a formal (written) succession plan? With whom?
- Is it funded?
- When was the last review?

9. Mergers and Acquisitions

- Do you plan to grow organically or possibly accelerate your business growth through mergers and acquisitions of other businesses?
- How do you locate acquisition opportunities?
- How do you know whether they are a good strategic fit and valued properly?

10. Financial Independence Planning

- What is your vision of financial independence and the quality of life you expect to have?
- What cash flow/asset modeling have you done? Are you on track?

11. Estate Preservation

- How do you intend to pass on your business at your death?
- Will your surviving spouse be OK?
- How will estate taxes be paid?
- What steps have you taken to reduce taxes? Have you done all you can?

12. Exit Strategy/Sale of Business

- When you started your business, did you have an exit strategy in mind?
- What is your current thinking relative to exit?
- What is the time frame?
- Will you sell? To whom? Will it be a 100 percent sale or just taking some chips off the table?

Now think about it: Which of the 12 points along the Value Path interest or concern you most at this time?

WHAT'S MY BUSINESS WORTH?

Determining business value is part science, part art, and part emotion, but some realistic techniques can be used to predict what the value range might be, giving consideration to all the tangible and intangible assets, current industry indicators, and current economic conditions.

Many different approaches exist to valuation, depending on the owner's objectives for the future of the business and, therefore, the purpose of performing a valuation. Since closely held businesses are not traded on a public stock market, the perspectives of the players matter.

Fair-Market Value

The IRS determines fair-market value under Rev. Ruling 59-60 as "the price at which the property [your business] would change hands between a willing buyer and a willing seller when the former is not under any compulsion to buy and the latter is not under any compulsion to sell, both parties having reasonable knowledge of relevant facts."

Most people believe the axiom that fair is fair, so the statement by the IRS is a reasonable summation of the principles of exchange as they relate to the nagging questions, "Did I get a fair price?" and/or "Did I settle for less than I should have?"

How Do You Get the "Right" Value?

The value of your business can be determined in a number of ways. Each method, in its own perspective, proves reliable, depending on the type of business, value of assets, technology considerations, and other factors specific to the value model.

In order to establish a baseline for value, a few methods are most commonly accepted in the business valuation process, lender calculations, and financial arena in general.

Earnings-Based Formulas (EBITDA)

One of the most common methods for determining business valuation is to calculate earnings before interest, taxes, depreciation, and amortization (EBITDA). The formula looks like this:

> **EBITDA** = gross revenue − business expenses (excluding interest, tax, depreciation, and amortization)

Many times, a capitalization rate, or a multiple, is applied to the EBITDA to determine the price that you would receive. For example, if EBITDA was $2 million and the multiple was 5, the value would be $10 million. For the sake of this discussion, assume that we are talking about a lower-middle-market business ($10–$100 million). This means that unless otherwise agreed to, all operating assets will be transferred and accounted for in the calculation.

Typically, in this calculation there may also be add-backs for items such as excess earnings of the owners, one-time capital expenditures, excess rent, and any other expenses that are nonrecurring or not necessary for the operations of the business—essentially hidden profit that would be available to the business (and a purchaser) otherwise. (See chapter 4, "Selling to an Outside Party for Maximum Value," for more on this.)

Which EBITDA Do You Use?

There are multiple variations of EBITDA, one of which will provide the highest potential value of your situation:

- ▶ **Reported EBITDA:** reflects your historical results.

- ▶ **Recast EBITDA:** includes the aforementioned add-backs.

- ▶ **Synergized recast EBITDA:** captures the synergies a potential buyer would realize as a result of purchasing your company. The additional profitability is extracted through cost savings as a result of economies of scale, increased market share, pricing, and so on.

This example shows a business that sold for six times EBITDA:

		Transaction Value
Reported EBITDA of $2 million	x6	$12 million
Recast EBITDA of $2 million	x6	$21 million
Synergized recast EBITDA of $5 million	x6	$12 million

An experienced M&A advisor or investment banker will represent your company to the marketplace, negotiate on the basis of the highest EBITDA, and fight for the highest multiple to arrive at the best price and terms.

See chapter 4, "Selling to an Outside Party for Maximum Value," for further discussion.

Other methods used to determine value are as follows:

- ▶ **Discounted cash flow (DCF):** In a DCF valuation, the value of your company is measured by estimating the expected future cash flows and then discounting those future flows by the desired rate of return in order to determine the present value of the future cash stream.

▶ **Capitalized earnings approach:** This approach measures the expected return on the buyer's investment.

▶ **Tangible assets approach (balance sheet items):** This approach determines the business value on the basis of total assets, or adjusted book value, which may be adjusted to the estimated fair-market value for the replacement cost of equipment or other assets.

▶ **Value of specific intangible assets:** This approach is generally used when the buyer sees value in a customer list, reputation, and so on, and the company has just a few tangible assets. This could also be called the goodwill of the business.

ACCESS TO CAPITAL

One of the greatest challenges business owners face in growing their business is access to capital. In today's economic environment, lenders are lending again, but qualification and security are tighter than ever. Whether financing is used to provide necessary working capital for current operations or fund growth or an exit strategy, the appetite for capital is omnipresent. It is important to understand how to raise capital beyond the founder's own money, family, and friends.

The likely first source, of course, is banks. Banks have a process to approve loans on the basis of their established loan policies, credit scoring, approval systems, and loan committees, and business owners need to know how banks approve loans before submitting applications. Various loan durations are available, matching the need with the useful life of the underlying collateral. Other popular loans include lines of credit that establish a maximum amount that can be borrowed, real estate loans, equipment loans, construction loans, and inventory loans.

Almost without exception, banks will require personal guarantees from the business owners or the largest stockholders. If traditional banks decline to lend, additional sources of borrowed capital include the following:

▶ Local, state, or federal governments (numerous programs exist, including the Small Business Administration [SBA])

▶ Asset-based lenders, who provide equipment loans, leases, and accounts receivable factoring.

These lenders take much greater risks than do traditional banks, and lending rates are commensurately higher.

Prior to an exit, an owner may wish to invest in his or her business for expansion, for value-building, or to refinance existing debt. It is important to have access to a national network of M&A advisors and investment bankers who specialize in raising senior debt, unitranche facilities, second lien debt, mezzanine financing, and equity capital for corporate clients. They should also have extensive experience raising debt and equity capital to finance leveraged buyouts, acquisitions, recapitalizations, refinancing, management buyouts, and shareholder dividends.

A process to satisfy your capital needs should include the following:

▶ Performing a comprehensive financial analysis of the desired transaction

▶ Helping you determine an optimal capital structure

▶ Creating a compelling offering memorandum

▶ Locating the right institutional lenders and investors

▶ Assisting with documentation and closing

The financing process involves many choices and requires multiple decisions. How these decisions are made is critical to the success of the transaction.

To get started, follow these steps:

1. Draft an executive summary of the financing project desired.

2. Why does your business need capital?

- Refinance existing debt

- Buy out a shareholder

- Support organic growth

- Fund an acquisition

- Create a partial exit (equity recap)

- Construction loan

- Bridge financing

- Real estate acquisition

- Other _____

3. Calculate the amount of funds requested. Do you want a:

   • Loan

   • Equity partner

   • Unsure

4. When are funds needed?

5. How will funds be used? Provide a detailed breakdown or a "Use of Funds" statement.

6. Financial justification: The following financial statements for the last three years are typically needed:

   • Balance sheet

   • Profit and loss statements

Once you've identified these variables, a skilled Business Intelligence Specialist working with your investment banking professional and other team members can contact the right lending sources and put together a competitive financing package for your consideration. This expert will approach various types of lenders, including banks and private equity.

Private Equity Groups

PEGs can be a good source of capital for businesses. They are pools of capital usually funded by money management firms, pensions, other institutions, and select high-net-worth investors. PEGs sometimes fund early-stage investments. Most often, they will fund growth-stage and late-stage businesses in need of mezzanine financing (subordinated debt layered between senior bank debt and equity) or buyouts in management-led transactions and leveraged recapitalization (the reverse of management buyouts, where management ownership is reduced). PEGs also, of course, acquire companies outright.

Private Placements: Debt and Equity

If you have experienced difficulty raising capital through traditional banking channels, you should consider alternative financing methods such as private placements.

A private placement of debt or equity is an option for private or public companies. In a debt-financed private placement, your company must have predictable cash flow to service the borrowings. In an equity private placement, you must have a thorough business plan and a strong, experienced team of managers.

Considerations for private placement include the following:

- Is your company enjoying strong growth?
- Does your company wish to raise capital to support such growth?
- Does your company need to finance an acquisition?
- Recapitalization: Do you seek liquidity but not a total sale of the business?
- Are public markets unsuitable as a result of offering size or other constraints?

EMPLOYEE BENEFITS

Another area important to your business's value path is the protection and cost-effectiveness of employee benefits programs.

Executive Benefits

Effective executive benefits are key to attracting and keeping your top talent. Here are some things you can do:

- Conduct a cost-benefit analysis of existing employee and fringe benefits. The best benefits are those that meet the needs of your employees.
- Determine if money spent now on company-wide benefits would better serve long-term goals by being reallocated.
- Review your current qualified plan to ensure you meet all ERISA §404(c) and other regulatory requirements.
- Determine if you meet the health care requirements that affect large businesses (50+ employees).
- What are the most competitive benefits that will attract and retain top/talented employees?
- Secure selective personal benefits and services with business dollars on a tax-favorable basis, wherever possible, to fulfill your personal needs as a business owner.
- Consider benefits that may help reward different tiers of your employees (i.e., top executives, middle management).
- Benefits could be designed as "golden handcuffs," which reward employees for staying long-term.

▶ Executive bonus plans and disability insurance are popular in terms of offering or expanding benefits.

Group Insurance

Insurance is another important factor for attracting and retaining valuable employees.

▶ Medical and prescription drug plans are most popular, and tend to be the first benefits brought on board; dental, vision, and life insurance are also frequently offered.

▶ Life insurance: These policies generally provide employees' survivors a death benefit in a set amount or an amount based on salary (e.g., two times salary). See chapter 6, "Protecting Your Business with Life Insurance," for more information.

▶ Disability insurance: These plans provide employees with an income stream, should they become disabled. Benefit amounts are typically a percentage of salary.

Retirement Plans

Many businesses offer some type of qualified retirement plan for owners and employees. Defined contribution plans are now the primary retirement savings vehicle for employees. 401(k)s are the most common type of retirement plan offered by all firms, regardless of size. 401(k) plans are followed in popularity by SEP, SIMPLE IRA, and Roth IRA plans, depending on the size of the business.

Which of the following types of retirement plans do you offer?

401(k) Plan

Employees may elect to defer receipt of income. The amount deferred consists of pretax dollars that are invested in the employee's plan account. As employer, you may match all or part of the employees' deferrals to encourage employee participation. The 401(k) plan is the most widely used type of retirement plan. 401(k) plans can also offer employees the opportunity to make after-tax Roth contributions.

Profit-Sharing Plan

This generally allows for some discretion in determining the level of annual employer contributions to the plan. In fact, your business can often contribute nothing at all in a given year if you so choose. The amount of contributions may be based on a written formula in the plan document, or may be essentially at your discretion. With a typical profit-sharing plan, employer contributions range anywhere from 0 to 25 percent of an employee's compensation.

Age-Weighted Profit-Sharing

Contributions are allocated based on the age of plan participants as well as on their compensation. This type of plan benefits older participants (generally, those having fewer years until retirement) by allowing them to receive much larger contributions to their accounts than those for younger participants.

New Comparability Plan

This is a variation of the traditional profit-sharing plan. This type of plan is unique in that its participants are divided into two or more classes, generally based on age and other factors. A new comparability plan can often allow businesses to maximize plan contributions to higher-paid workers and key employees and minimize contributions to the other employees.

Money Purchase Pension Plan

In this plan, you as employer make an annual contribution to each employee's account. The amount is determined by a set formula that cannot be changed, regardless of whether your business is showing a profit. Typically, your business's contribution will be based on a certain percentage of an employee's compensation.

Target Benefit Plan

This is a hybrid of a defined benefit plan and a money purchase pension plan. It resembles a defined benefit plan in that the annual contribution is based on the amount needed to fund a specific amount of retirement benefits (the "target" benefit). It resembles a money purchase pension plan in that the annual contribution is fixed and mandatory, and the actual benefit received by the participant at retirement is based on his or her individual balance.

Defined Benefit Plan

This guarantees the employee a specified level of benefits at retirement (for example, an annual benefit equal to 30 percent of final average pay). As the name suggests, it is the retirement benefit that is defined, not the level of contributions to the plan. The services of an actuary are generally needed to determine the annual contributions that you must make to the plan to fund the promised benefits. Contributions may vary from year to year, depending on the performance of plan investments and other factors. Defined benefit plans allow a higher level of employer contributions than most other types of plans, and are generally most appropriate for large companies with a history of stable earnings. Defined benefit plans are generally funded solely by the employer.

Cash Balance Plan

This type of plan has become increasingly common in recent years as an alternative to the traditional defined benefit plan. Though it is technically a form of defined benefit plan, the cash balance plan is often referred to as a "hybrid" of a traditional defined benefit plan and a defined contribution plan. This is because cash balance plans combine certain features of both types of plans. Like traditional defined benefit plans, cash balance plans pay a specified amount of retirement benefits. However, like defined contribution plans, participants have individual plan accounts for record-keeping purposes.

Simplified Employee Pension (SEP) Plan

This is a tax-deferred retirement savings plan that allows contributions to be made to a special category of IRAs, according to a specific formula. Generally, any employer with one or more employees can establish a SEP plan. With this type of plan, you can make tax-deductible employer contributions to SEP-IRAs for yourself and your employees (if any). Except for the ability to accept SEP contributions from employers (allowing more money to be contributed) and certain related rules, SEP-IRAs are virtually identical to traditional IRAs.

SIMPLE IRA Plan

The Savings Incentive Match Plan for Employees (SIMPLE) is a plan for small businesses (generally those with 100 or fewer employees) and self-employed individuals that is established in the form of employee-owned IRAs. The SIMPLE IRA plan is funded with voluntary pretax employee contributions and mandatory employer contributions. The annual allowable contribution amount is significantly higher than the annual contribution limit for traditional and Roth IRAs, but less than the limit for 401(k) plans.

SIMPLE 401(k) Plan

This is a qualified retirement plan for small businesses (generally those with 100 or fewer employees) and self-employed persons, including sole proprietorships and partnerships. Structured as a 401(k) cash or deferred arrangement, this plan was devised in an effort to offer self-employed persons and small businesses a tax-deferred retirement plan similar to the traditional 401(k), but with less complexity and expense.

A Savings or Thrift Plan

Similar to a profit-sharing plan, this has features that provide for (and encourage) after-tax employee contributions to the plan. The employee must pay tax on his or her own contributions before becoming invested in the plan. Typically, a thrift/savings plan supplements after-tax employee contributions with matching employer contributions. Many thrift plans have been converted into 401(k) plans.

Caution: If you provide any type of retirement plan to employees, keep the following in mind and review your plans accordingly.

Question	Concern
When did you last conduct a comprehensive review of your 401(k) plan to make sure internal expenses are in line with the market?	Plans that are three years old or older and have not been reviewed are at risk of being overpriced.
When was the last time you conducted a review of the investment lineup to ensure it is meeting the objectives of the plan?	Fund lineups need to be reviewed for compliance with your investment policy statement (if one exists) and the meeting of plan objectives. Approximately 70 percent of businesses have plans that have not been "benchmarked"; that is, they have not been compared with industry indices in order to track performance results.
Are you or your plan sponsors concerned about the personal liability associated with being a fiduciary of a plan?	Breach-of-fiduciary responsibility could lead to personal liability of plan sponsors, usually an owner, CFO, or other executive serving in that role.
How are you fulfilling your fiduciary responsibilities as they relate to the selection and ongoing monitoring of the plan fund lineup?	Many plan-level fiduciaries do not understand their responsibilities with regard to fund selection and ongoing monitoring and are unaware of the resources available to assist with these responsibilities.

How are you protecting yourself from personal liability as it relates to the investments at the participant level?	Plan sponsors can be held personally liable for participant losses due to breach-of-focus liability if participant-level investments are not outsourced effectively.
What steps are you taking to ensure all fiduciary responsibilities are being fulfilled from an ongoing plan administrative perspective?	Many plan sponsors do not understand their responsibilities and are unaware of the resources available to assist with these responsibilities.

These concerns are real.

During fiscal year 2011, the Department of Labor closed more than 3,472 civil investigations. More than 75 percent of the plans were required to restore losses to the plan or take another type of corrective action to correct plan deficiencies. Enforcement efforts for fiscal year 2011 resulted in the collection of a staggering $1.38 billion through plan restorations, fines, and penalties *(Source: Department of Labor, 2011)*. The DOL is getting even tougher today.

BUY/SELL AGREEMENTS

All too often, owners with partners or co-shareholders (co-owners are called members in an LLC) do not have a written plan in place to deal with the continuity of their businesses. A business has far greater value as a going concern sold to your surviving partner(s) than could be realized upon its liquidation. Without a plan, you may not have the time or the bargaining power to receive maximum value for the business.

Nothing assures that a purchaser can be found who will buy at a price and on terms satisfactory to owners and their families, especially if such a sale must be made quickly at an emotional time. A buy/sell agreement creates a market for closely held business stock that otherwise would be difficult for owners or their families to sell. Families' financial security will otherwise be threatened, with business owners' salaries cut off and the uncertainties of a sale negotiation. In addition, provisions are often not made for the payment of taxes that may be due upon transfer. Survivors may be forced to liquidate the business at a price substantially below fair-market value.

In summary, the lack of a business agreement may bring the following consequences:

- ▶ It may fail to set a fair price for the business or may encourage disagreement and delays at the worst possible time. Cash is not guaranteed in order to buy the interest of a deceased, disabled, or retired partner.

▶ It allows the IRS to contest the value and thereby potentially increases the estate for estate tax purposes.

▶ In the event of the death of one of your co-owners, you may have to do business with one of your former co-owner's relatives, who has little or no knowledge of your business. Alternatively, if you want or need to buy out the deceased co-owner's survivor, the value and terms are uncertain.

▶ In the event of the death of one of your co-owners, you may have to accept your co-owner's relative's sale to an outsider to recoup the share. You could be in for the challenge of your life.

▶ In the event of the death of one of your co-owners, important management decisions could be delayed. Heirs of owners have very different concerns but still retain their voting rights.

▶ In the event of the death of one of your co-owners, you may wind up doing all of the work while sharing the profits equally.

▶ In the event of the death of one of your co-owners, you may seek capital to meet additional expenses but with a substantially weakened credit rating.

▶ In the event of the death of one of your co-owners, you could be forced to operate with credit temporarily cut off because the bank wants to "wait and see," or because outstanding loans and/or lines of credit may be called.

▶ The business may suffer irreparable loss in the period between the termination of your service and the completion of a sale.

▶ Additional tax and administrative costs may severely limit the net dollars received from your business interest.

KEY EMPLOYEE RETENTION AND INCENTIVE PLANS

One of the most important factors impacting a buyer's decision to purchase and pay high value for a business is the strength and quality of management. Buyers want to ensure the following:

▶ **Capability:** Management is capable of running and growing the company.

> ◗ **Commitment:** Key management is committed to executing the plan and forecast. Long-term employment contracts are in place.

> ◗ **Relationships:** The customers and suppliers will continue to do business on the same terms with the company after ownership change.

To that end, retaining key, high-value employees is critical to the future success of your closely held businesses. Business succession planning by private employers poses unique challenges in contrast with public companies. In a highly competitive environment for talent, the ability of private owners to attract, retain, and motivate senior executives is critical in defining the success of any organization.

> **Your key employees and managers may be your company's biggest assets. What special incentive programs are in place to motivate them to grow your business and remain long-term?**

Key Person Insurance

The death of a key employee can cause serious problems for your business. After all, in today's economy, the competition for top-level talent can be as fierce as the competition for customers. To protect against this loss, at least from a financial perspective, your business can acquire a life insurance policy on the life of the key employee(s).

The business entity owns the policy and pays the premiums. The company has all rights to the policy's living benefits, such as access to the cash values if a permanent policy is used. Death proceeds are received income-tax free. The life insurance proceeds received by the company can be used for a variety of purposes, including attracting and compensating replacement talent.

Many guidelines can be used to determine the dollar value of a key employee. These include a multiple of the person's compensation, estimating profits lost, or the replacement methods as examples.

Sound planning should examine all of the methods to determine the appropriate amount of insurance coverage needed to insure the key employee. These include the following:

> ◗ **Contribution method.** How much is the key employee contributing to the profits of the company?

> ◗ **Replacement method.** What will replacing the key employee cost?

▶ **"Five years of salary" method.** Calculating five years of salary provides a rule-of-thumb formula to value a key employee.

Retaining Key Employees with Deferred Compensation

Supplemental executive retirement plans, which fall in the arena of *nonqualified* deferred compensation (NQDC) plans, are instrumental in leveling the playing field for private companies when competing with public companies for senior executives. Public companies rely on equity-based benefits extensively, which is a handicap at private companies. In this regard, NQDC plans serve an increasingly important role in enhancing executive benefits packages at private companies that cannot be provided with *qualified* plans.

The many benefits of implementing a NQDC plan include the following:

▶ Attracting, retaining, and motivating senior executives

▶ Avoiding distribution of stock as compensation

▶ Controlling cash compensation costs

▶ Competing with public companies offering alternate forms of benefits

▶ Aligning the interests of the executives with those of the employer

▶ Maintaining full discretion to determine eligibility for participation

▶ Offering complete flexibility in deciding how to informally fund the plan's obligations

▶ Maximizing the sale price of the company by locking in senior management

▶ Rewarding long-tenured senior executives at the time of sale of the business

From an executive's perspective, the benefits of a NQDC plan offered by their employer include the following:

▶ A financially secure, tax-deferred retirement supplemental benefit in addition to taxable cash compensation

▶ A form of benefit in lieu of equity-based benefits

▶ The ability to participate in the financial success of a company as a non-owner

Government limits on tax-qualified retirement programs severely restrict the ability of employers to offer comprehensive retirement benefits from qualified plans. Some of these restrictions include limits on the maximum compensation that can be taken into account in qualified plans and limits on employer contributions to defined-contribution plans.

As a result of government limitations, highly compensated executives face a form of reverse discrimination, whereby their retirement income from qualified plans is proportionately much less than that for lower-compensated employees. In addition, a greater percentage of final compensation is required in order to retire comfortably. For private employers, the deficiencies of qualified plans can thus be addressed only by implementing Supplemental Executive Retirement Plans (SERPs) to supplement executive retirement income and for retention purposes.

Plan designs are highly customizable, allowing employers to deliver benefits commensurate with their needs. In general, plans are designed in either of the following two key configurations:

1. **Nonqualified defined-benefit (DB):** This plan provides the participant a specified percentage of final average compensation, similar to a pension plan. The employer has considerable flexibility in specifying what benefit amount is to be provided, whether by a formula or as a specific dollar amount. The employer also has the option to fund the future liability informally by utilizing mutual funds, institutionally priced life insurance, and the like. A key characteristic of a DB is that the employer is subject to the investment risk, since the benefit to the participant is specified.

2. **Nonqualified defined-contribution (DC):** With this plan the employer makes specified annual contributions into a participant's account on the basis of a formula or metrics designed by the employer. In this case, the employer may also informally fund the obligation by utilizing a funding vehicle. On the basis of the initial annual rate of return assumptions, the contribution amounts are predetermined, but the final benefit amount to a participant may vary. The participant is usually given some control over the investment choices for the account. Under this type of plan, the participant is subject to the investment risk, since the benefit received at retirement is dependent upon the performance of the selected investment options.

> **A NQDC plan allow private employers to compete with public employers.**

Nonqualified deferred compensation plans allow private employers to compete with public employers by implementing a valuable succession-planning vehicle. Given their many advantages, they are widely utilized by private employers to attract, retain, and motivate senior executives.

CHAPTER SUMMARY

Entrepreneurs often spend the better part of their adult lives nurturing and growing a business. They take on significant risk because they are passionate about their ability to compete in the marketplace and win

You don't get a "do-over." You get one chance to do it right.

on the basis of their ideas, products, and services. Their companies survive and thrive as they evolve through their life cycles, known as the *value path*.

Typically, phases along the value path are described as the *early stage*, *growth stage*, and *late stage*, culminating in the owners' point of exit. The majority of business owners are in the growth to late stages. You probably are, too. During this critical period, it is important that you address the key factors that are necessary to continue your upward track—especially if you're planning for your optimal One Way Out.

Unfortunate events along the way can impact your business's value. You therefore must plan for the potential disability, death, or retirement of the owner(s), as well as the creation and funding of buy/sell agreements, nonqualified deferred compensation plans, qualified retirement plans, and asset protection strategies.

Factors affecting your business's value as it grows include access to capital, your employee benefits, executive benefits, and retirement plans. There are many variations of these—401(k) plans, profit-sharing plans, targeted benefit plans, defined benefit plans, SEP IRAs, and others—giving you the opportunity to find the optimal fit for your company's profile and goals. If you haven't taken a recent look at your company's retirement plan, it may be time for a checkup, considering these questions:

1. Has the plan gone through a comprehensive benchmarking process within the last two to three years?

2. Has the plan pricing been updated within the last two to three years?

3. Has the plan failed to meet any testing requirements in the past?

4. Does the plan currently carry the appropriate coverage from a fidelity bond perspective?

5. Has the fund lineup changed or been reviewed within the last 12 months? Is the current fund lineup 404(c) compliant?

6. Does the current plan provide offer 3(21) and/or 3(38) fiduciary services within the plan?

If you answered NO or I DON'T KNOW to any of these questions, your plan may benefit from a checkup.

The art and science of retaining key employees is also exceedingly important for growing value. That's because in today's economy, the competition for top-level talent can be as fierce as the competition for customers. To protect against the loss of key employees, at least from a financial perspective, your business can acquire a life insurance policy on the life of each one of these most valuable assets.

You also can retain key employees through deferred compensation plans. These also are called supplemental executive retirement plans, and are instrumental in leveling the playing field for private companies when competing with public companies for senior executives.

As your business progresses in its evolution, you need to measure its value. Many different approaches exist for doing this, depending on your objectives for its future. These include fair market value, as well as earnings-based formulas. One of the most common methods for determining business valuation is to calculate earnings before interest, taxes, depreciation, and amortization (EBITDA) and multiply by an industry-specific multiple, as a starting point. There are numerous value drivers and value enhancers and other factors to consider that were more fully described in chapter 4, "Selling to an Outside Party for Maximum Value."

Orchestrating these essentials in order to attain the best results requires well-considered, strategic planning and execution. Working with a qualified Business Intelligence Specialist and a team of professional experts, you will achieve success in all of these areas and maximize your business's growth along the value path.

See the Growing and Protecting Your Business checklist at
www.YourOneWayOut.com.

Chapter 6

Protecting Your Business with Life Insurance

LAST YEAR, TWENTY MILLION PEOPLE bought quarter-inch drills. Not a one of them wanted a quarter-inch drill; they only wanted what the quarter-inch drills could provide: quarter-inch holes. That's similar to life insurance. No one wants life insurance, but savvy business owners want what it can do. Just consider these questions:

- What would your family receive for your business if you died yesterday? Is that number what you really think your business is worth?

- How will your buy/sell agreement terms be carried out? Will the cost of buying out your partners at death or disability deplete all of the company's cash?

- How much revenue does your business generate? How much business value is attributable to the talents and efforts of your key people?

- Is it important to retain your key people until you exit, or beyond? What would be the financial impact of losing a key employee?

- If you don't give your key employees and top executives the benefits they deserve, will your competitors?

- What special benefits do you offer key employees beyond a paycheck and the same benefits given to rank-and-file employees?

These are uncomfortable scenarios to face, but they warrant answers to protect the value of your business. All are critical components of your One Way Out plan.

Human capital drives the success of a business. What will result if you or one of your partners or key management personnel dies or becomes disabled and his or her expertise is lost? Or what will happen if a key employee leaves your company to work for a competitor or strike out on his or her own? It happens all the time.

IN TODAY'S ECONOMY, THE COMPETITION FOR TOP-LEVEL TALENT CAN BE AS FIERCE AS THE COMPETITION FOR CUSTOMERS.

I work with a business that lost three executives in a two-year period. One loss was due to a heart attack, another due to an automobile accident. A third key person was severely injured in a skiing accident and was unable to return to work for three years due to chronic back pain and medication issues. The business suffered significantly.

MANAGING THE RISK

Managing this sort of human capital risk is essential for your eventual successful exit from the business, but is there a way to do it cost-effectively? The answer is yes: these contingencies can be mitigated through the use of documents such as buy/sell agreements and deferred compensation/golden handcuffs plans, along with key-man life and disability insurance to protect your company from loss.

Life insurance can, in fact, provide many benefits for your business, playing a key role in solving the following issues:

- Buy/sell agreement funding
- Succession planning
- Retirement solutions
- Extraction of equity from business
- Nonqualified retirement plans
- Retention of key employees
- Debt indemnification

Details on the structure of many of these tools can be found in chapter 3, "Choosing Among the 5 Exit Paths." Life insurance also is an important tool for the estate planning and wealth preservation topics covered in chapter 7, "Defending Your Wealth."

CONTINGENCY PLANNING

Life insurance can play an important role throughout each stage of a business's value path, as illustrated in Figure 6.1. It allows you to plan for contingencies, mitigating risk using company dollars, while offering numerous benefits. These include the following:

- Providing your family with financial security if you die prior to your planned exit date.

- Allowing the business to continue with minimal interruption to customers.

- Providing for orderly transfer of business to successors.

- Eliminating the issue of nonparticipating spouse or family members obtaining ownership through a buy/sell agreement with your co-shareholders.

- Making funds available for the payment of estate taxes and administration costs.

- By funding a buy/sell agreement, guaranteeing a market for stock and thereby avoiding a forced sale.

- Eliminating the payment of income tax by the estate on the sale of the business at death and providing tax-free cash to make the purchase.

- Avoiding the need for borrowing to pay the purchase price.

- Avoiding disturbance in the financial and competitive position of your business.

- Providing a tax-advantaged retirement planning vehicle for owners and key employees. Policy cash values can be used to fund deferred compensation retirement benefits paid to executives. Death benefits can be used as cost-recovery mechanisms for the company.

- Motivating key employees without offering real equity in the business, by using life insurance to create "synthetic equity plans."

- Providing for repurchase of ESOP shares. Many employee stock ownership plans (ESOPs) require the company to repurchase the shares upon the death of an owner/employee. Life insurance can help provide the funding dollars for this obligation.

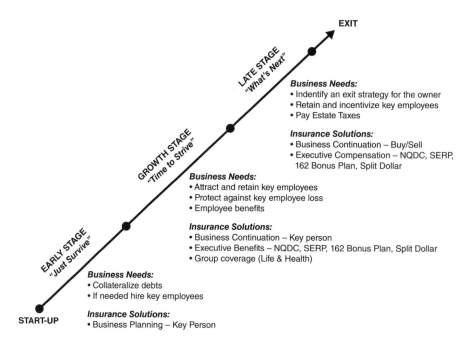

Figure 6.1. Life insurance plays an important role in each stage of the value path.

▶ Creating additional liquidity to avoid a forced sale of family assets.

▶ Creating estate equalization among heirs, particularly when specific assets (such as business interests) are designated for particular heirs.

▶ Addressing multiple marriages and providing for children from more than one spouse.

BUY/SELL AGREEMENT FUNDING

Buy/sell agreements are described in chapter 3, "Choosing Among the 5 Exit Paths." To summarize, these documents help a business to do the following things:

▶ Identify a purchaser of the business (other shareholders or the company itself).

▶ Establish and define the "triggering" events. These include death, disability, retirement, divorce, bankruptcy of a shareholder, loss of professional license, and other voluntary and involuntary terminations.

▶ Establish the method for determining price/value.

▶ Specify the payments term (i.e., number of years, interest rate, etc.).

▶ Address the funding method: Will the company use its own cash, borrow from a bank, or rely on future earnings and cash flow to make buy-out payments?

Life insurance is often the most cost-effective and tax-efficient way to fund the obligations of a buy/sell agreement. Premiums may be paid for by the business.

FUNDING A STOCK REDEMPTION PLAN

Life insurance can be used to fund a stock redemption plan. Here's how it works:

▶ A stock redemption or *entity purchase agreement* spells out what would happen if a triggering event, such as death or disability of an owner, occurs. The owners agree to sell their ownership interests back to the company upon the triggering event.

• Life insurance is purchased on each owner in an amount equal to the value of their ownership position in the business. With a stock redemption plan, the business is the owner, beneficiary, and premium payer of the policy.

• At death, life insurance proceeds are paid directly to the business. The death benefit is received income tax–free. (However, watch for potential exposure to alternative minimum tax (AMT) if your business is a C corp.)

• The estate sells the business interest back to the company. The business pays the estate of the owner who dies an amount equal to the value of the ownership position in the business. Additional coverage may have been purchased as "key person" coverage, which would provide the business with a cushion to offset the loss of the owner.

• With the use of a permanent life insurance policy, the cash value of the policy can be used to provide funds in case of retirement or other lifetime termination of the owner.

While term insurance will provide a death benefit, the use of permanent life insurance can provide funds for other types of buy-outs when death does not occur prematurely. The cash value from the policy can be accessed in a tax-efficient manner, providing dollars to buy out a living shareholder, or at least provide a meaningful down payment.

Advantages

- Cash value of policy is an asset of the business.

- Simple and easy to administer.

- Premiums are paid for by the business, which equalizes the premium payments across owners.

Disadvantages

- Policies and cash values may be subject to business creditors.

- If business is a C corp, surviving owners receive no increase in tax basis of percentage of business redeemed. If business is a pass-through entity, such as an S corp or LLC, survivors may receive close to a full basis step-up in basis, if properly handled.

Funding a Cross-Purchase Plan

In this scenario, a cross-purchase agreement is drawn up so that the surviving owners agree to *personally* purchase the business interests of the other owner(s) in the event of a triggering event. Here's how it works:

- The owners establish a cross-purchase buy/sell agreement. Owners agree to purchase the interest of any owner upon a triggering event (e.g., death).

- Each owner buys a life insurance policy on each other owner in an amount sufficient to fund a buyout based on the value of the owner-ship position in the business. Each business owner is the owner and beneficiary of the policy (or policies).

- The company may pay for premiums under a bonus arrangement (IRC Sec 162) or split-dollar arrangement.

- When an owner dies, the life insurance proceeds are paid directly to the surviving owner(s)/beneficiary(ies). Death benefits are received income tax–free. The money is then used to purchase the business interests from the deceased owner's estate.

- The estate of the deceased owner will receive the proceeds of the sale income tax–free. The stock value receives a step-up in basis at the decedent's death. Provided the transaction takes place in a timely manner, the estate realizes no capital gain and no income tax is due.

Advantages

- Cash value and policy are generally not subject to the creditors of the business.

- Surviving owners receive a full step-up in basis in stock purchased from estate of deceased owner. This minimizes future capital gains taxation when survivors sell stock.

- Minimal taxes due on sale of stock for heirs.

Disadvantages

- Cash value and policy are not assets of the corporation, and therefore cannot be shown on books.

- Policies are subject to individual's creditors.

- Premiums are paid from personal funds, and may be disproportionate since younger owners must buy and pay premiums for those who are older. Note: A business can pay premiums under a bonus or split-dollar arrangement.

- It may be cumbersome to purchase and administer the policies if there are many owners.

Funding a Wait-and-See Plan

Consider a buy/sell agreement today that addresses all of the contingencies while providing maximum flexibility for the business and its owners. With a wait-and-see buy/sell agreement, only one thing is left for future determination: identification of the purchaser. Everything else is put in place, drafted, executed, and defined. However, the identification of the purchaser, whether it is the company or the surviving owner(s), is left open and addressed through a series of rights of refusal.

At the time of a triggering event, such as death, the survivors and their advisors can determine who the optimal purchaser should be. If the tax laws at that time favor a cross-purchase, then that is what will be chosen. If the tax laws favor a stock redemption (entity purchase), then that approach will be taken. This is typically accomplished through a series of rights of refusal that expire after perhaps 30 days, and then move on to the next option:

- Option to purchase is given to the company.

> Option to purchase is given to other owners personally.

> Obligation of the company to purchase.

The sequence of options is *critical.* Otherwise, payments will be considered dividends.

The insurance may be owned several ways:

> By the owner(s) personally (similar to a cross-purchase): If a redemption is chosen, the owners can loan the insurance proceeds to the company to effectuate the purchase.

> By the business: Insurance proceeds payable to the company can be used to purchase if a redemption is chosen. Alternatively, if a cross-purchase is utilized, the business may loan insurance proceeds to owners so they can personally buy the entity interest.

> By irrevocable trusts: Insurance proceeds paid to trusts may be loaned to the purchasing party to effectuate the desired buy-out arrangement.

Funding Disability Scenarios

Even if you are careful to draft and fund a buy/sell agreement that spells out the disposition of the business at your death, while providing the resources to carry out the plan, there is still one more involuntary event to be addressed. What happens in case of a disability? Does the disabled owner get bought out, or does a disabled owner continue to draw salary, take bonuses, share profits, vote on decisions, and own the company indefinitely? Some buy/sell agreements do not even address disability, and even if they do, oftentimes owners do not take the steps to cost-effectively fund them.

It is important to acquire disability buyout (DBO) and disability income (DI) coverage when you are young and healthy, since your chances of being disabled increase over time.

Key Elements to Consider

> *Definition of disability:* How disability is defined in the agreement is very important and should coordinate with the definition in the disability insurance policy.

Note: An important reason to acquire disability insurance is to insert an independent party to define whether a shareholder is disabled or not. This becomes especially problematic for a rapidly growing business with a shareholder who becomes very sick or hurt but wants to maintain ownership, whereas the "nondisabled" shareholders want to buy that shareholder out because he or she may no longer contribute to the future growth of the company. An insurance company is an adverse third party that will not pay a claim unless it qualifies under the policy's definition of disability. This may reduce disagreement and potential lawsuits over this issue.

- ▶ *Elimination period:* The period of time between the first day of the disability and the trigger date. Periods of 12 months to 24 months are common options.

- ▶ *Trigger date:* This is the date at the end of the elimination period when the buyout begins and the insurance company begins paying on the policy.

- ▶ *Successive disability:* A disabled person may temporarily return to work but thereafter have a recurrence of disability. In many plans, successive disability periods can be tied together to meet the elimination period.

- ▶ *Funding period:* The period over which the buyout payments are made. It can be an immediate lump sum or spread out over a period of months, or a combination of both. The funding period set in the policy should match the terms of the buy/sell agreement.

- ▶ *Recovery from disability:* The recovery of a disabled person after the buyout has begun can raise several questions, among them: Does the funding stop? Can the person return to work with the same company? Lump sum settlement plans, in some cases, can remove some of the uncertainty.

- ▶ *Involvement in the business:* Many insurers require that the business owner be actively involved in the business prior to disability.

EXECUTIVE COMPENSATION FUNDING

"Take away my factories; take away my railroads, my ships, my transportation; take away my money; strip me of all these, but leave me my men and in two or three years, I will have them all again." – ANDREW CARNEGIE

As discussed in chapter 3, "Choosing Among the 5 Exit Paths," a vital component in protecting and growing your business along the value path, ensuring that you achieve your optimal One Way Out, is the retention of your key employees. These are your most valuable players—those who have the managerial acumen and customer relationships that contribute a significant portion of your business value. In a competitive world, you can give them a strong incentive to stick around with executive compensation and risk-management programs. These can be supported with financial and tax advantages through the use of business insurance.

Funding an Executive Bonus Plan

A properly structured executive bonus plan can be a powerful tool for recruiting, retaining, and rewarding key employees. It also can be a way to help employees save for retirement and provide financial protection for their families.

> **Compensation is more than a paycheck! Executive benefits can be an effective way to retain and incentivize key people.**

With this plan, also known as an Internal Revenue Code Section 162 Bonus Plan, the employer and employee enter into an agreement under which the employer agrees to pay an annual bonus equal to the premium on a permanent life insurance policy with cash value (see Figure 6.2). The executive or a third party, such as an irrevocable life insurance trust (ILIT), can own the policy. Here's how it works:

- The executive applies for and purchases a life insurance policy on his or her life and designates a personal beneficiary. Alternatively, the executive may gift the bonus to his/her ILIT and the ILIT's trustee can purchase the policy.

- The employer pays and tax-deducts the bonus payment. The executive reports the bonus as ordinary income. The bonus can be paid to the executive or directly to the life insurance company.

- At retirement, the executive may elect to access the policy's cash value via a series of withdrawals and loans. If properly structured, these withdrawals and loans can be income tax–free.

- Ultimate death proceeds are received income tax–free by the beneficiary. If paid to an ILIT, proceeds will also be free of estate taxation.

Employer Advantages

- Enhances executive compensation package.

- Selective participation allowed. You can pick and choose who participates and how much to contribute.

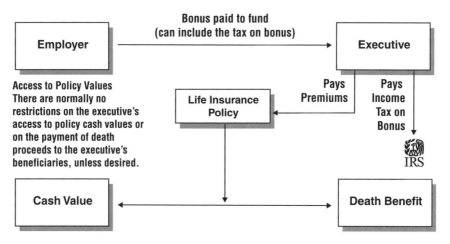

Figure 6.2: An executive bonus plan can be funded by life insurance.

◗ Simple to install.

◗ Minimal cost to implement.

◗ Company receives immediate tax deduction.

Employee Advantages

◗ Low-cost life insurance.

◗ Significant rate of return on tax cost when measured against cash value.

◗ Immediate vesting.

◗ Employee owns policy.

◗ Can name beneficiary, typically family or trust.

◗ Can access policy's cash value to supplement retirement income.

KEY PERSON INSURANCE

Key person insurance is a life insurance policy purchased by an employer on the life of a highly valued employee (or owner) to help protect the business as beneficiary from the financial loss resulting from that employee's death. Policy proceeds can be used to recruit, hire, and train a replacement.

THE COST OF LOSING VALUED EMPLOYEES CAN RANGE FROM TENS OF THOUSANDS TO HUNDREDS OF THOUSANDS OF DOLLARS IN LOST PROFITS AND BUSINESS VALUE.

Basically, key person insurance is coverage that can provide a cash cushion for the business in the event of an untimely death of a key employee and can help creditors, other employees, customers, and shareholders remain comfortable about the business's long-term stability and viability.

Determining the Amount of Key Person Coverage

The amount of coverage needed depends on what the business stands to lose at the death of the key person. There are a number of valuation methods utilized in assessing this loss, predicated on the following factors:

▶ Loss of business value.

▶ Loss of excess earnings.

▶ Cost to replace employee.

▶ Cost to replace lost sales or profits.

▶ Multiple of salary.

Supplemental retirement income and family protection is very important to valued employees.

▶ Amount of bank debt, lines of credit, mortgages, or other lender obligations that may come due if the person who guarantees the loan dies. **Note:** Most obligations become "callable" in the event of death and change of ownership.

With key person insurance, the business is the owner, pays the premiums, and is the beneficiary.

NONQUALIFIED DEFERRED COMPENSATION PLAN FUNDING

A business and/or an employee may elect to defer future income (and taxation) through various types of deferred compensation arrangements. The basic concept is shown in Figure 6.3.

	Employer	Key Employee
Agreement	Agrees to pay compensation for a set period after a stated date or death.	Agrees to continue service until specified date (e.g., normal retirement age). Optional: After separation, agrees not to compete and/or to provide consultation services.
Advantages	Employer retains key employee.	Employee (or heirs) receives extra retirement benefit when tax bracket may be lower.
Taxation	Benefits paid to employee (or heirs) are deductible to employer when paid or constructively received.	Benefits are taxed when payments are made or constructively received.

Figure 6.3. A nonqualified deferred compensation plan rewards and retains your key employees.

How It Works

Under this plan, the business agrees to pay compensation for a set period after a stated date (such as retirement age) or death. The key employee agrees to continue service until a specified date and also could be offered a noncompete provision. The employee then can receive a supplemental retirement benefit as an incentive for long-term service. Benefits may be linked to performance (i.e., increasing sales or profits) to provide a reward for achievement of company goals. This could certainly have a positive impact on increasing business value for your exit. (See Figure 6.4.)

Here are some key items to remember about a nonqualified deferred compensation plan:

▶ Unlike "qualified retirement plans," such as 401(k) plans, pension plans, and the like, a nonqualified plan can discriminate. The employer can pick and choose which employees to benefit. Various amounts may be contributed and paid out.

▶ Deferral must generally be agreed upon before the compensation is earned.

▶ If the plan is unfunded, the compensation is not taxable until received.

▶ If the plan is funded, the employee's rights must be subject to substantial risk of forfeiture and they must be nontransferable. If they are not subject to such risk or are transferable, the payments become currently taxable.

▶ A cash-value life insurance policy can be used to "informally" fund an agreement. It can provide the necessary funds at either death or retirement.

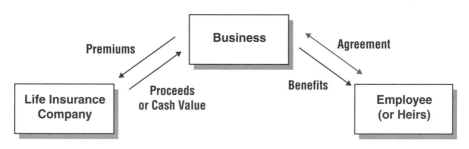

Figure 6.4. A nonqualified deferred compensation plan informally funded with life insurance has advantages for businesses and their key employees.

- Nonqualified plans are not subject to the pre–age 59½ distribution penalties or the age-based mandatory distribution rules imposed on qualified retirement plans.

- Take care to meet the requirements of IRC Section 409A, as failure to comply could result in immediate taxation, a 20 percent penalty, and an underpayment interest penalty. The scope of 409A is far-reaching and complex. It can be a trap to the unaware. Consult an advisor familiar with the rules to ensure compliance.

Why is life insurance advantageous in a nonqualified plan?

- It is self-completing. If the key person dies, tax-free life insurance death benefits are payable to the company and/or the key employee's named beneficiary.

- Life insurance cash values are not subject to income taxes. The "inside buildup" of interest, dividends, and capital appreciation are not taxable.

- Cash value withdrawals (up to basis in policy) and loans are tax-free.

SPLIT-DOLLAR PLANNING STRATEGIES

A split-dollar insurance arrangement can be very useful in funding business needs such as buy/sell agreements, nonqualified deferred compensation arrangements with key employees, and key person indemnification to the business, as well as a strategy to minimize income, estate, and gift taxes.

A split-dollar plan allows a business to assist an employee (or owner) with the purchase of needed life insurance protection by paying all or a portion of the premiums. Cash values and death benefit also are split between two parties. It leverages company funds, and cash value can provide deferred compensation on a tax-efficient basis. All of this makes it a win–win situation for the employer and the employee.

Employer Advantages

- It can be an effective method of attracting and retaining valuable key employees.

- The employer may have access to the policy's cash value.

- The employer can be highly selective regarding which employees are covered.

▶ Under certain ownership arrangements, the cash value stays on the company's balance sheet as an asset.

▶ The arrangement does not need IRS preapproval.

Employee Advantages

▶ Split-dollar can provide needed personal life insurance protection at a reduced current out-of-pocket cost.

▶ Policy cash value becomes a source of supplemental retirement income.

▶ Split-dollar can be combined with a cross-purchase buy/sell agreement among business owners to even out the premium cost in the case of a wide age variance.

There are two main methods, or regimes, of split-dollar plans today, known as the *economic benefit regime* and the *loan regime*. Whatever party owns the policy determines how the policy is taxed.

Economic Benefit Regime

Under the economic benefit regime, the company owns the policy and endorses a portion of the death benefit to the employee or his or her trust. The premium is split between its economic benefit (the cost of term insurance) portion and the balance. The economic benefit for income and gift tax purposes can be significantly lower at younger ages because it is based on the annual "term" cost of the death benefit and not the policy's full premium. This is especially advantageous for estate-planning purposes.

Loan Regime

Under the loan regime, the employee is the owner of the policy with a collateral assignment made back to the employer to repay the loan. The company (non-owner) of the life insurance policy, the lender, makes a series of loans, along with interest charges, on all or part of the premiums to the policy's owner, the borrower. Each loan will bear interest at the applicable federal rate (AFR) or higher.

The employee repays the loan either during his or her lifetime using a portion of the policy's net cash value and other available funds or at death using the life insurance proceeds.

Economic Benefit Regime / Endorsement Split-Dollar

An economic benefit regime/endorsement split-dollar plan, as illustrated in Figure 6.5, is an agreement between an employer and an employee to split the cost of a life insurance policy on the employee's life. This arrangement is ideal for business owners and key employees, ages 45 to 65, who want to leverage corporate dollars to purchase life insurance for a retirement supplement, survivor needs, estate planning, a key person, or a buy/sell agreement.

Economic benefit regime/endorsement split-dollar arrangements vary according to the wording of the actual document used in each situation. A Split-dollar arrangement can be customized to accomplish different goals.

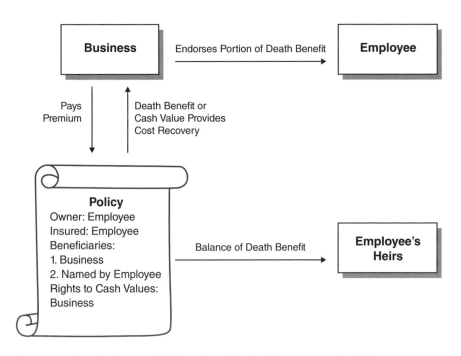

Figure 6.5. A typical economic benefit regime/endorsement split-dollar arrangement.

Loan Regime / Collateral Assignment Split-Dollar

A loan regime/collateral assignment split-dollar plan is an agreement between an employer and an employee that helps fund a life insurance policy owned by the employee. It is cost-effective and may be particularly advantageous to older business owners or key employees because, as with endorsement split-dollar plans, loan interest may be less than the economic benefit.

In a loan regime/collateral assignment split-dollar arrangement (see Figure 6.6), the employee is the owner of the policy. The employee also owns the rights to the policy cash values. The business receives its portion of the death benefit through a policy assignment, with the remainder going to the employer's named beneficiaries. Thus the employee can receive a valuable life insurance policy at a reduced cost.

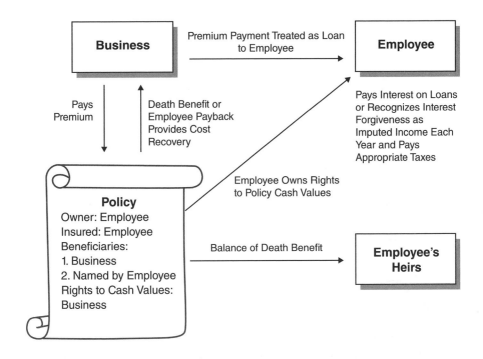

Figure 6.6. A typical loan regime/collateral assignment split-dollar arrangement.

[1]*Loan Regime/Collateral Assignment Split-dollar arrangements vary according to the wording of the actual document used in each situation. A Split-dollar arrangement can be customized to accomplish different goals.*

Joint Ownership Split-Dollar

A unique form of split-dollar involves joint ownership of a policy between a business and key employee. (See Figure 6.7.) Through a joint ownership agreement, both the employer and the key employee share in the policy's benefits, values, and privileges in a carefully prescribed manner. Joint ownership provides several distinct advantages:

▶ Balance sheet "friendly": It creates an asset without a bookable liability. Also, company-owned cash value may be pledged, borrowed, or assigned.

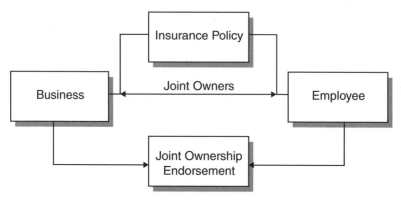

Figure 6.7. Joint ownership split-dollar plan.

▶ The employee is protected against potential claims of the company's creditors.

▶ No postretirement obligations on the part of the employer.

▶ No Department of Labor or Employee Retirement Income Security Act (ERISA) reporting requirements or limitations.

▶ Gradual tax deduction over employee's working career, rather than waiting until retirement.

▶ Manageable tax cost, if any, by employee during working career.

▶ Employer controls transfer of ownership, which can be based on performance.

CASE STUDY: RETAINING A KEY PERSON

Here's an example of how a joint-ownership split-dollar plan effectively solves the need for key person insurance and provides a nonqualified deferred compensation benefit to retain and reward a key employee.

Staygrow, Inc. has a valued employee, Joe Keyman. Joe is 43 years old and has been with Staygrow for 10 years. His current annual salary is $150,000.

Goals

Under this plan, Staygrow and Joe own the policy jointly at first, with Joe gradually assuming full ownership. Upon retirement, Joe controls the tax-free distributions from the policy, achieving the following goals for both parties:

- ▶ Joe receives a supplemental retirement income of $75,000 per year for 15 years

- ▶ Staygrow maintains cash value on balance sheet for 22 years.

- ▶ Staygrow provides a preretirement death benefit for Joe's wife and children in case he dies prematurely.

- ▶ Staygrow receives a key person death benefit if Joe dies while in the company's employ.

Structure

Staygrow's structure for this arrangement is shown in Figure 6.8.

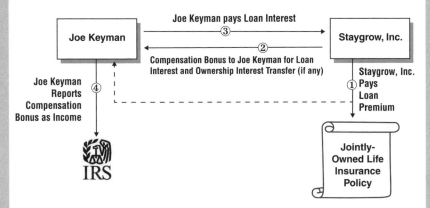

Figure 6.8. Example of how a joint ownership split-dollar plan works.

Staygrow's Results

Staygrow, Inc.'s financial results from this arrangement are shown in the following table:

Staygrow, Inc. Annual Premium	$17,114
Total Premiums	$376,524
Net Outlay (total premium less tax savings @ 34%)	$243,506
Initial Death Benefit payable to Staygrow, Inc.	$300,000

Joe is projected to receive policy with cash value at age 65 of $666,061. He may generate a supplemental retirement income benefit of $75,000 per year from the time he is 65 through age 80 through tax-free withdrawals from the policy. If he dies prior to collecting all of his distributions, his family will receive a tax-free death benefit.

Joe Keyman's Results

Joe's specific financial results under this arrangement are shown in the following table.

Initial death benefit to Joe's heirs	$390,000
Joe's Cash Surrender Value at age 65*	$666,061
Joe's Cumulative Outlay	$143,519
Rate of Return at the end of Joint Ownership* (age 65)	19.61%
Annual cash flow generated from age 65 thru 80	$75,000
Total Cash Flow ($75,000 x 15 yrs.)	$1,125,000

* Projected @ 6.58% indexed interest, not guaranteed.

This example is for illustration purposes only. Actual results will vary based on your specific situation. Consult your own tax and/or legal advisor(s) when making tax and legal decisions. Any values are hypothetical examples only, not guarantees. A personalized basic life insurance illustration is required that includes product features and any guarantees.

EVERY BUSINESS NEEDS CPR

If your company owns or pays for life insurance to support any of the aforementioned strategies, a corporate policy review (CPR) is recommended at least every three years.

Today's life insurance policies tend to be superior to those that were issued years ago. Insurance companies have become leaner, meaner, and more competitive; life expectancies have increased, resulting in lower mortality costs; and technology has driven down the cost of issuing and servicing policies, in addition to many other improvements.

Prolonged low interest rates and increasing reserve requirements have negatively impacted many policies. This has caused an immediate need for business owners to revisit their corporate policies and goals from both a personal and a holistic business perspective.

THE BOTTOM LINE IS THAT LIFE INSURANCE IS NO LONGER A BUY-AND-HOLD ASSET. IT MUST BE REVIEWED REGULARLY, JUST LIKE YOUR INVESTMENT PORTFOLIO.

That's why your business needs a corporate policy review (CPR). Economic conditions, including an ever-changing array of regulations, have made it prudent to review your policies for both performance and compliance considerations.

A CPR program provides business owners and their financial, legal, and accounting advisors with observations and recommendations that allow them to make informed decisions with regard to their company's life insurance and the plans to which those policies relate (i.e., buy/sell agreements, split-dollar, key person, deferred compensation plans, estate plans, etc.).

Review your existing life insurance at least every three years for the following things:

- Guaranteed and nonguaranteed elements of permanent policies
- Sufficient death benefit amounts and length of coverage
- Adequate funding/premium levels
- Appropriate type of policy (i.e., temporary or permanent)
- Cost and/or benefit analysis
- Appropriate ownership structure and beneficiary designations
- Policy loans that might affect premiums, cash values, and/or death benefits adversely
  - Ensuring that the need still exists and the policy adequately meets those needs
- Compliance with tax laws such as IRC Section 101(j), which applies to policies issued after August 17, 2006, in which a business is the owner and beneficiary of the policy and an employee is the insured. There are a few exceptions to the law, but if an exception is not met and the insured employee did not provide written consent *prior to issue of the policy* and the business failed to report to the IRS on Form 8925, then the death benefits are subject to income taxes when paid to the business.

Changes in the insurance industry can also affect your corporate life insurance policy in these ways:

- Reduction in the dividend scale or interest crediting rate.

- The current prolonged low-interest-rate environment creates strains on the insurance companies for investment options, increased reserve requirements, and restrictions of lump-sum premium deposits and leads to underperformance of existing policies.

- Due to these low interest rates, some carriers may increase cost of insurance for existing universal life policies. This may result in the need for higher premiums.

- Sporadically funded or underperforming contracts may be in danger of lapsing.

- "Vanishing-premium" and "quick-pay" scenarios acquired in the past are in danger of lapsing and/or being overloaned, creating detrimental tax consequences.

- Regulatory impact (AG 38) increased reserve requirements for guaranteed death benefit contracts.

- Changes in the tax and legislative environment (e.g., new regulations on older split-dollar arrangements have affected all such policies and may need to be restructured or rescued).

- Term insurance should be reviewed to makes sure conversion costs (to a permanent form of insurance) are competitive.

Auditing Your Policies with an In-Force Ledger

At least every three years, you should request and analyze an *in-force ledger*—a written confirmation directly from your insurance company on the status of your policies in force. This is a critical component to the CPR process.

Requesting the in-force ledger will allow you to establish a baseline with which you can compare the current policy to the original policy illustration created when the policy was issued and to options available in the marketplace today. This is critical because it allows you and your advisors to evaluate and comparison shop your current policies, then upgrade if the benefits of new policies exceed those offered by your current holdings.

Three premium scenarios are needed in every policy audit situation:

1. The originally illustrated premium structure, including lifetime distributions to be made, if any

2. The premiums necessary to maintain the coverage to age 100

3. Consideration of how policy will perform if no additional premiums are paid.

Be sure to request that these scenarios are calculated at:

▶ current dividend or interest rates;

▶ 100 to 200 basis points (1 percent to 2 percent) lower than the current rate; and

▶ *guaranteed* dividend or interest rates.

This is the only accurate way to measure policy performance. Lack of CPR may result in unpleasant surprises that could cost your company thousands, possibly millions, of dollars in lost benefits or wasted premium dollars.

If your existing policy is not performing as expected, or if needs have changed, consider alternatives to correct the policy (i.e., increase the premium amount, reduce the death benefit, etc.). If the result is still unsatisfactory, consider other policies available in the insurance marketplace.

Possible Reasons to Exchange or Replace a Policy

Following are common reasons to consider the exchange or replacement of an older policy (this list is not all-inclusive):

▶ **Lower-cost, more competitive plans are now available:** In any market, improvements are inevitable, and prices tend to decrease because of new innovations. Over time, insurers have cut expenses and distribution costs. When this is combined with other pricing improvements, it can lead to much more competitive policies, with lower costs and/or features and benefits not available on earlier plans.

▶ **"Excess cash value":** Some older policies have accumulated hundreds of thousands—sometimes millions—of dollars in cash value. In certain cases, the cash value can be exchanged for a new, superior policy with significantly higher death benefits and perhaps lower premiums and stronger guarantees.

▶ **Guaranteed Death Benefits:** A desirable policy design feature for certain universal life policies includes the ability to guarantee the death benefit based on a fixed-premium structure. This guarantee applies even if interest rates experience a sustained drop or the current cash value declines or disappears. The real benefit to this type of policy is that the insured can be assured that his or her death benefit will always be guaranteed, as long as the premium is paid according to schedule.

▶ **Better mortality:** Along with dramatic improvements in medical science comes a corresponding increase in life expectancy. Because of this, many new policies have lower mortality expenses than existing policies do—sometimes significantly lower.

▶ **Preferred and preferred-plus underwriting:** When universal life was introduced twenty-five years ago, only two classes of standard underwriting were available: smoker and nonsmoker. Since that time, these classes have been subdivided into preferred and, in some instances, even preferred plus. This occurred first for the nonsmoker class and later for the smoker class. If you fall into one of the preferred classes, you might benefit from the lower mortality charges in an exchange.

▶ **Special underwriting programs:** If currently "rated" and paying a higher premium due to medical problems and the existing company won't remove the rating, you could possibly qualify under a special underwriting concession program with a different insurer. This is a program where rated cases will automatically be issued a standard, lower-priced classification. If health has improved from a previous rating, you might benefit from a program like this.

▶ **Company strength:** One of the most important factors a business should consider is the strength and stability of the issuing life insurance company. Companies that are highly rated possess an improved ability to keep their promises to their policy owners.

▶ **Loan treatment:** Having a significant loan on a policy may seem insurmountable, but this doesn't have to be the case. Under the 1035 exchange rules, the IRS allows for the transfer of a loan, along with the cash value, from an existing life insurance policy to another life insurance policy, so long as the insured and the owner are the same. Some insurance policies offer attractive loan interest rates that might not be available on the existing policy. A *wash loan* may even be an option, meaning that interest credited on the loan amount is the same as that charged for it. This could be important if you do not plan to pay back the loan. Another potential benefit is the ability to use cash withdrawal to completely or partially pay back the loan.

◗ **Extended maturity:** Many existing policies have an age 85, 90, or 95 maturity date. When a policy matures, the policy cash values will become payable to the owner of the policy, and taxes will be due on any gain. The insurance contract will be completed, so the death benefit will not be paid. Newer policies can extend the maturity date into the future to avoid this debacle.

CHAPTER SUMMARY

As an essential element in your One Way Out plan, business life insurance can play an important role in each stage of your value path, protecting your company when used for the following purposes:

◗ Funding for buy/sell agreements, whether a stock redemption plan, cross-purchase plan, or wait-and-see plan

◗ Funding an executive bonus plan

◗ Covering the loss of key employees

◗ Funding a deferred compensation plan

◗ Extracting equity from the business while minimizing taxes

◗ Providing nonqualified retirement plans

These and other life insurance applications can be executed using your business's dollars through a wide variety of arrangements, such as bonus or split-dollar plans. With these, the company pays all or a portion of the premiums, with cash values and death benefit split between two parties—the company and the employee. This approach leverages company funds and cash value to provide deferred compensation, or to fund a buy/sell agreement on a tax-efficient basis.

There are various methods of designing the right split-dollar arrangement for your business needs:

◗ Economic benefit regime

◗ Loan regime

◗ Endorsement method

◗ Collateral assignment

◗ Joint ownership

Each arrangement has different advantages to your business and your employees. The ideal design is based on the purpose of the coverage.

Life insurance also allows you to plan for contingencies, mitigating risk using company dollars, again while offering numerous tax benefits. These types of uses include the following:

- Tax-advantaged retirement planning. Policy cash values can be used to fund deferred compensation retirement benefits paid to executives. Death benefits can be used as cost-recovery mechanisms for the company.

- The repurchase of ESOP shares. Many employee stock ownership plans (ESOPs) require the company to repurchase the shares upon the death of an owner/employee. Life insurance can help provide the funding for this obligation.

- Corporate split-dollar loans to key employees. You can offer low-interest rates to acquire life insurance on an income tax–advantaged basis.

- Cash value accumulation and policy loans to avoid higher income taxes and the Medicare net investment income tax surtax.

You, your company, your trust, or a third-party lender such as a bank can pay the life insurance premiums. Financial leverage, as well as tax leverage, can make the life insurance transaction even more financially appealing.

However, life insurance is no longer a buy-and-hold asset. Policies have changed over the years, as have general economic conditions, regulations, and, no doubt, your business profile and objectives. Prolonged low interest rates and increasing reserve requirements have negatively impacted many policies. This has caused an immediate need for business owners to revisit their corporate policies along with the business arrangements and agreements they support.

For all of these reasons, your company needs a corporate policy review (CPR) at least every three years. This process results in observations and recommendations that will allow you and your financial, legal, and accounting advisors to make informed decisions about the effectiveness of your company's life insurance policies and the plans or strategies they support.

The CPR process should address these key considerations:

- Existing company-owned insurance policies should be reviewed to ensure they are still performing as expected and will provide the liquidity, protection, and desired cash proceeds.

▶ Executive benefits plans that were put in place to recruit, reward, and retain top talent should be reviewed at least every three years.

▶ Buy/sell planning is another area business owners should review. Having prefunded, up-to-date plans in place can allow owners to transition out of the business in the time frame they have in mind and at the value that meets their needs.

Your CPR should include a review of an in-force ledger directly from the insurance carrier, calculated under multiple scenarios, to ensure that the policies are expected to perform and accomplish their intended purposes. If not, corrective action needs to be taken. Fully utilizing and regularly reviewing your business's life insurance profile will assure that you are positioned optimally for your One Way Out.

See the Corporate Policy Review checklist at <u>www.youronewayout.com.</u>

Chapter 7

Defending Your Wealth

AN ESSENTIAL ELEMENT OF THE ONE WAY OUT process is wealth preservation. This coordinates your business succession and wealth distribution plans. No plan is complete without preserving and passing on the wealth you have worked so hard to achieve, whether it is the business itself or the reinvested proceeds from a liquidity event. In fact, the exit planning process often begins with preparation of wealth preservation documents and funding to protect the family if the owner exits prematurely. Don't put this step off until your exit plan is concluded.

I cover the topic of wealth preservation more fully in my previous book, *Defend Your Wealth*, but this chapter will provide you with the essentials that you will need to support your One Way Out plan.

AS A BUSINESS OWNER, WHAT DO YOU NEED TO KNOW ABOUT WEALTH PRESERVATION, ESTATE AND GIFT TAXES?

As unpleasant as estate planning and wealth preservation are to some, it is a necessary part of your holistic One Way Out plan. No one likes to face their own mortality, the possibility of incapacity as they age, the threat of the IRS forcing liquidation of 40 percent to 50 percent of their net worth, or potential attacks from predators and creditors seeking to confiscate dollars from them, their children, or their grandchildren. But without a proper, up-to-date wealth preservation plan, this nightmare can become a reality.

WHAT SHOULD A WEALTH PRESERVATION PLAN DO?

A wealth preservation plan will help accomplish your objectives in the following areas:

- Provide for your surviving spouse and other family members in the event of your demise.

- Provide that assets will be managed properly if you become disabled or incompetent.

- Distribute your assets, including your business if you own it at the time of your death, in accordance with your wishes after you (and later, your spouse) are gone.

- Protect assets from predators and creditors (yours, and those which your children and grandchildren may someday face).

- Maximize use of all applicable Internal Revenue Code deductions, exclusions, and tax credits to save taxes.

- Make sure that your family pays the absolute minimum amount of income, gift, estate, and generation-skipping taxes (GST).

- Ensure that your charitable intentions are met.

- Provide for an equitable distribution of assets among your children, especially if you have children who are actually involved in your business and others who are not. (Note: equitable does not necessarily mean equivalent dollar value, just a distribution plan that meets your definition of "fair.")

- Objectively review your existing legal documents, such as wills, trusts, powers of attorney, living wills, health-care directives, prenuptial agreements, divorce decrees, and so on.

- Review the ownership and beneficiary designation of life insurance policies and qualified retirement plans to minimize tax consequences and make sure they flow to whom you want, when you want, and in the proper amounts.

- Develop a prearranged plan for the management and expenses associated with long-term care.

A wealth preservation plan should be customized to meet any special needs you or your family may have and should anticipate both the good things and the bad things that could happen in the future.

THE FIVE PHASES OF WEALTH PRESERVATION

So how do you make the wealth preservation process as painless as possible? How do you keep from getting bogged down or overwhelmed? You take one step at a time.

As shown in Figure 7.1, I break wealth preservation planning down into five phases:

- ◗ Fundamental
- ◗ Basic
- ◗ Intermediate
- ◗ Advanced
- ◗ Charitable (Zero Estate Tax)

Don't jump over any phases without completing them in order.

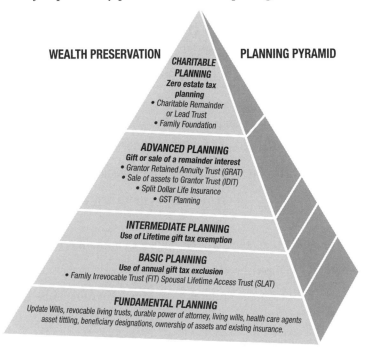

Figure 7.1. Wealth preservation can be broken down into five phases.

PHASE 1—FUNDAMENTAL PLANNING

When I meet a business owner for the first time and request a copy of his or her will (as part of the document audit portion of One Way Out Process Step 1—Discovery), I am often amazed by what I read. There is no mention of the owner's business! The owner's single largest, most important asset is not addressed. In fact, it looks like the same will written for a corporate executive or retiree. Essentially, all assets pass (often outright) to the surviving spouse, if any, and then to *all* children equally as an outright distribution at certain ages.

WHAT'S WRONG WITH THIS PICTURE?

This may appear to be perfectly acceptable on the surface, since all assets are transferred to the surviving spouse upon passing. However, it poses a host of tax, distribution, and asset protection threats:

- No asset protection.

- No protection in the event of a second marriage.

- No assurance that assets will pass to your children.

- No ability to have professional asset management assistance from a trustee.

- Is the surviving spouse a US citizen? If not, the ability to transfer assets to spouse tax-free is severely limited.

Other problems associated with basic wills that threaten your family wealth include the following:

- Assets subsequently passing outright to children.

- Children leaving assets outside of family.

- Exposure to their potential creditors and predators.

- Inclusion of assets in children's taxable estates before passing to grandchildren.

Assets left to children *outright* will be subject to numerous hazards:

- The potential claims of a divorcing spouse

- The potential claims of children's creditors (lawsuits, auto liabilities, malpractice, bankruptcy, etc.)

- Estate taxes when assets are left to the next generation (i.e., grandchildren)

▶ Gift taxes, should they try to give away the assets they have inherited to your current or future grandchildren while living

The takeaway in all of this is that you have to be careful to create the proper wills and trusts. As a starting point, you will need to create up-to-date core estate documents and coordinate asset titling, beneficiary designations, and ownership of existing life insurance policies. The number of high-net-worth families who, unfortunately, have not executed even this fundamental level of planning or have not updated the documents that do exist would amaze you.

"MY ATTORNEY WROTE A WILL FOR MY SPOUSE AND ME—IS OUR WEALTH PRESERVATION PLAN DONE?"

Is a will an estate preservation plan? How about a revocable living trust, power of attorney, or life insurance policy/trust to pay estate taxes? These are all individual *ingredients* of wealth preservation. An effective plan is personal to you. It should not be boilerplate, or the same as your neighbor's or the past ten people who saw the same attorney as you.

Once it's done, can you put it in a drawer and forget about it? Not on your life! Wealth preservation plans change constantly as a result of internal dynamics (e.g., family, net worth, new objectives) and external forces (e.g., tax laws, economic conditions, etc.).

Estate Taxes

Estate taxes are the single largest threat to the transfer of businesses and other wealth in this country. You work your entire life to earn a buck. You lose roughly 50 cents to various income taxes (federal and state), leaving 50 cents out of every dollar to live on and invest. Those 50 cents

> **Estate taxes are the single largest threat to the transfer of wealth in this country.**

will manifest themselves in savings, investments, and business or real estate assets that are taxed again at 40 percent to 50 percent upon your death. This is the ultimate in "double taxation." Property subject to income and estate taxes can be taxed twice.

If you look at your estate in its entirety (100 percent), you actually own and control the disposition of 60 percent of your assets. The US Treasury and state taxing authorities have a "lien" on the other 40 percent above the exemptions, and they are waiting patiently to collect it.

Most business owners are unaware of the dollar amount of the estate taxes that will be levied upon their estates after their demise—neither are they aware that the IRS demands cash payment of these taxes, generally within nine months of death! There are provisions of the Internal Revenue Code that allow installment payments; however, estates must qualify and interest must be paid on any outstanding estate tax liability. A forced sale of your most valuable assets or highest-income-producing property or the loss of control of a family business will result from not having enough cash when it is needed most. Worse still, forced sales—because they may yield pennies on the dollar to pay the full-priced tax bill—only compound the impact of failing to address one's estate preservation needs.

After more than a decade of confusion, Congress finally acted to bring greater certainty to the estate tax law. The American Taxpayer Relief Act of 2012 (ATRA of 2012) reunified the state and gift tax exemptions. The $5 million exemption (indexed annually for inflation) for estate taxes, gift taxes, and generation-skipping transfer taxes became permanent. The top estate tax rate increased from 35 percent to 40 percent.

As of 2016, individuals with estates over $5.45 million (or $10.9 million in the case of a married couple) are subject to estate taxes. These exemptions from estate taxes will increase each year with the consumer price index (CPI). Your life expectancy (and your spouse's) may be another 20, 30, or 40 years. Who knows what your net worth will be, or what tax rates and exemptions will be in place at that time? Consider the steps our country may need to take in order to address a nearly $20 trillion and growing deficit and other fiscal woes. It won't be pretty.

Under the current laws, taxable estates will be subject to a tax of 40 percent on value above the inflation-adjusted estate exemption amount. If you live (or die) in a state with a state-level inheritance or estate tax, then you will owe that amount in addition to the federal tax.

A/B Testamentary Trusts

A/B testamentary trust plans require the execution of a will and/or revocable living trust, which, at death, optimizes tax exemptions by dividing the deceased spouse's probate assets into two portions: a credit shelter (a.k.a., bypass) trust and a marital trust.

The credit shelter trust is funded with the amount that can pass free of federal transfer taxes at both spouses' deaths, currently $5.45 million for 2016, and indexed in future years. The trust may be held for the benefit of the entire family. Often, we recommend that our clients consider keeping the credit shelter trust in continuing trust and use discretionary (not mandatory) distributions of trust assets to give their family access to these family assets while providing asset protection and management assistance.

The marital trust is funded with the balance of the deceased spouse's probate estate. This is held for the *exclusive* benefit of the surviving spouse, who *must* receive all trust income. We often recommend that our clients keep the balance of the marital trust in a continuing qualified terminable interest property (QTIP) marital trust for the surviving spouse, and use discretionary (not mandatory) distributions of trust principal to provide for the surviving spouse. Assets passed down through the marital, or QTIP, trust are generally subject to estate taxes when the surviving spouse dies.

Asset Titling

Because no one can predict which spouse will die first, to help optimize each spouse's exemption, we advise retitling enough assets into each spouse's individual name to provide for the optimum use of the estate tax and generation-skipping exemptions available to each at death. Jointly titled assets will not work for this purpose. For 2016, $5.45 million should be retitled into each spouse's separate name. As the exemption increases through indexing, additional assets should be retitled. Most high-net-worth families should not rely on portability.

The concept of portability allows any unused exemption to be passed to a surviving spouse. The idea is to eliminate the need to retitle assets and establish complex wills and trusts (e.g., QTIP, credit shelter, bypass, or family trusts). The unused exemption is called the "deceased spousal unused exclusion amount," or DSUEA.

There remain many compelling nontax reasons to continue use of A/B trust wills and proper asset titling between spouses in estate plans. Surviving families require asset management, parents require assurance that assets will pass to their children and not to subsequent spouses, professionals require asset protection from civil suits, blended and nontraditional families have special needs, business interests must be continued, and incapacity planning often can best be accomplished with such trusts.

It is ill advised to rely solely on the portability of the federal estate tax exemption to plan a large estate, as many states have their own state death taxes and virtually all states are continually seeking new sources of income in a financially challenging economy. Portability does not apply to generation-skipping transfers. For example, a surviving spouse cannot receive the deceased spouse's unused generation skipping tax (GST) exemption.

Other reasons not to rely on portability include the following:

▶ The deceased spouse's credit is not indexed for inflation; therefore, it doesn't shelter future asset growth.

▶ Affirmative action is required when a spouse dies. An estate tax return (form 706) must be timely filed. If not, portability is not possible. Failure to file could become a major fiduciary issue in the future.

If the surviving spouse is sued, assets are exposed to creditors. If the spouse dies, the estate elects portability, the surviving spouse remarries, and his or her second spouse predeceases him or her, the exemption could be lost. This could inadvertently cost the family millions of dollars in unnecessary estate taxes.

I also recommend that the following additional estate preservation documents be created (or updated) to protect you and your wealth:

▶ Durable power of attorney

▶ Living wills

▶ HIPAA release and authorization

Life Insurance Ownership and Beneficiary Pitfalls

Much confusion surrounds the proper ownership and beneficiary arrangement of life insurance policies. In all my years defending clients' wealth, I have never seen the IRS named as a direct beneficiary of a life insurance policy on an application. However, this is, in essence, what happens every day as a result of lack of proper planning. Again, the tendency with married couples is often to name their spouse as the beneficiary of a life insurance policy.

> **I have never seen the IRS named as a direct beneficiary.**

Many individuals are the owner of their policies. This is the way most insurance is written in the United States today, and it has been traditionally owned this way. When it comes to planning for high-net-worth individuals, this arrangement is entirely unacceptable because this type of life insurance ownership and beneficiary designation inadvertently makes the IRS the beneficiary of 40 percent of the insurance proceeds upon the passing of the surviving spouse.

Most people are shocked by this discovery because they believe that life insurance is tax-free. In fact, it may be *income tax–free* under the Internal Revenue Code. However, when the insured (or spouse) owns the policy, the policy's death proceeds are includible in his or her taxable estate. This tax problem also applies if a company or another entity controlled by the insured owns the policy.

For example, if you own a $1 million policy, in essence, you are paying premiums for $1 million of life insurance coverage but are receiving only $600,000 of net proceeds. No client I've ever met is okay with paying one and a half times the premium amount he or she should for life insurance.

Some other consequences of incorrect life insurance ownership include the following:

▶ Children potentially could be disinherited. What if you die and your spouse receives the insurance proceeds and then remarries? Through no fault of your own, your children may be disinherited IF your spouse dies before his or her new spouse. In that case, assets would pass to the new spouse and then under that person's will, to whomever he or she designates (possibly not your children and grandchildren).

▶ Children or grandchildren (at age 18 or 21) could inherit unnecessarily taxed life insurance proceeds in a lump sum.

▶ Assets are not protected from the surviving spouse's creditors and, ultimately, children's creditors and potential divorce.

▶ Professional asset management of proceeds is lacking for the family.

Qualified Retirement Plan Taxation

Another area of major concern for high-net-worth individuals is the taxation of their qualified retirement plans and IRAs at death. People establish qualified retirement plans such as pensions, profit sharing, 401(k)s, and IRAs to provide for their future retirement income and to defer income taxes as long as possible. These are admirable goals. However, the IRS levies significant penalties for keeping money in such plans for too long and deferring distributions

Qualified retirement plans and IRAs may well be the best place to accumulate wealth while you are alive, but they may be the absolute worst place to own assets when you die.

and attempting to use these vehicles as a way to pass on wealth to children and grandchildren. Most people wait until required minimum distributions are necessary at age 70½ before taking money out of their traditional (non-Roth) retirement plans.

Because of the substantial value of assets held in qualified retirement plans and IRAs, they will trigger significant income and estate taxation upon death. These qualified retirement plans and IRAs may well be the best place to accumulate wealth while you are alive, but they may be the absolute worst place (for tax purposes) to own assets when you die.

PHASE 2—BASIC PLANNING

Basic planning is the next phase in your wealth preservation plan. It extends the previous phase of planning by creating a lifetime plan to reduce your taxable estate through annual exclusion gifts, either outright to family members or into estate-tax-exempt trusts.

Annual Exclusion Gifts

An individual donor can annually give up to $14,000 (in 2016) to any other individual free of transfer tax liability (of course, the receipt of the gift is not taxable income for the donee). This $14,000 can be combined (or split) with a gift from the donor's spouse to the same donee, to double the amount transferred to $28,000 per year. The donor and spouse may make annual exclusion gifts to any number of donees during a given tax year. The amounts are indexed to inflation.

For example, if you have three children, two daughters-in-law, and three grandchildren, for a total of eight possible donees/beneficiaries, you can make split gifts to each family member or a trust for their benefit, resulting in a gift-tax-exempt transfer of $28,000 × 8 beneficiaries = $224,000 each and every year.

Start with the idea of making gifts to reduce the size of the taxable estate. This can best be explained with the "tax fence" concept.

Figure 7.2 illustrates this concept, with includable assets shown on the left side of the tax fence. Assets shown on the right side of the fence are in a vehicle, such as a family income trust, and will pass tax free to family members. Assets can be transferred from the left side to the right side of the fence by making gifts and taking advantage of the annual gift tax exclusions and lifetime exemptions.

TAX FENCE CONCEPT

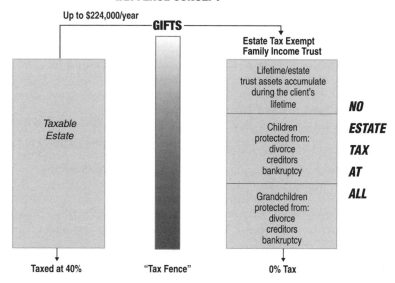

Figure 7.2. Tax-includable estate assets are shown on the left side of the fence; estate-tax-exempt assets are on the right.

Bottom line: Every dollar you transfer over the fence puts an additional 40 to 50 cents in your heirs' pockets and can provide multigenerational asset protection!

What can you give away? Just about any asset you own:

- Stock in your closely held business
- Real estate
- Marketable securities
- Cash
- Retirement plan distributions (you must distribute cash and pay income taxes first)

So why doesn't everyone do this? *Concern over affordability.* Again, remember, "Are we OK?" No one wants to compromise their standard of living in order to minimize future estate tax exposure. Therefore, you need to create and analyze your financial independence models (before and *after* contemplated gifts, to make sure that you and your spouse will continue to be OK).

NOW IS YOUR ONCE-IN-A-LIFETIME OPPORTUNITY!

PHASE 3—INTERMEDIATE PLANNING

The next phase in preserving your wealth, intermediate planning, involves a proactive plan to utilize your lifetime gift tax exemption by transferring assets out of your taxable estate to reduce future estate taxes and protect assets inside various trusts.

Most business owners have done very little, if any, proactive lifetime planning to reduce the estate tax bite Uncle Sam will inevitably take. For instance, how much of your $5.45 million lifetime gift tax exemp-

> **This year will bring about a bonanza of activity to avoid future taxation.**

tion have you already used to transfer business interests, real estate, or other assets to a trust to avoid estate taxes? If married, have you also utilized your spouse's $5.45 million exemption? If not, read on …

ATRA of 2012 created an unprecedented opportunity for lifetime wealth transfer. The law sets the 2016 gift, estate, and generation-skipping transfer (GST) tax exemption at $5.45 million per person ($10.9 million per couple), indexed for inflation going forward. The increase in the gift tax exemption means that you have an opportunity to transfer a significant number of assets (e.g., business, real estate, securities, etc.) out of your taxable estate so that all future appreciation escapes estate and generation-skipping transfer taxes (GST)—that is, it is not taxed to your grandchildren and future generations after your children have passed.

This is all great news, especially in a relatively low-interest-rate environment. It is the perfect storm for wealth preservation planning. We continue to witness a bonanza of planning activity to avoid future taxation.

THE WORST THING TO DO IS NOTHING!

Be mindful of the statute of limitations. When a gift is made of company stock, real estate, or other assets, it is important to file a gift tax return to start the clock running on the IRS. It can be challenging to place a value on certain asset transfers, so the sooner the value is determined and the return is filed, the sooner the three-year period begins. If properly disclosed and the IRS does not question the value after three years, it stands.

The $5.45 million exemption ($10.9 million for a married couple) is not a family heirloom. If you can afford to do so, you should consider transferring some or all of the credit during your lifetime. You pay a significant tax penalty by waiting until you die to use this credit, because all of the appreciation in value is included in your taxable estate.

Let's assume that you can afford to use your gift tax exemption now, instead of waiting until you die. If you transfer $5.45 million of assets out of your estate today, under the rule of 72 and an assumed 6 percent growth rate, the amount would double every 12 years. If you live 12 years after the transfer, the assets will have grown to $10.9 million; in 24 years, they will be worth *$21.8 million;* in 36 years, they will be worth $43.6 million; and so on.

Therefore, as a result, the actual amount transferred tax free would be $43.6 million, not just $5.45 million. That is a potential tax savings of more than *$16.8 million,* since the $43.6 million would have been included in your taxable estate.

> **The time to take advantage of these strategies is now.**

I can't emphasize enough that the time to address this is NOW. Future legislation may reduce the amount of the lifetime gift tax exemption, or may reduce the availability or effectiveness of certain techniques.

The "Endangered Species" List

Certain popular planning techniques may disappear in the near future due to new budget bills likely to be passed by Congress. These include the following:

▶ **New limits on gift exclusions.** For several years, budget proposals have created a new category of transfers, which includes transfers to trusts, pass-through entity gifts, and certain restricted transfers. If enacted, these proposals would impose an annual limit on how much would qualify for the annual gift tax exclusion of $50,000 per donor on such transfers. Individuals using annual exclusion gifts to fund insurance trusts and to make gifts to family members may need to consider alternative funding arrangements, should laws be enacted with these limitations. Outright annual exclusion gifts would remain available.

▶ **Valuation discounts among related parties (family).** Currently, a discount can be claimed on assets transferred to family members (or trusts for their benefit) through a gift or bequest for reasons such as lack of control or lack of marketability. Often these discounts can approach 30 to 40 percent of the asset's value. Proposed regulations are expected to be issued under Section 2704 of the Internal Revenue Code to reduce the ability to claim such discounts, which would restrict the amount of wealth transferred and increase tax liabilities.

‣ **Grantor retained annuity trusts (GRATs) may change.** Currently, you can set up short-term GRATs, for as little as two years, or extremely long-term (e.g., 99 years) GRATs to minimize gift tax exposure. The reason for doing this is to derive a small gift amount, based on present value calculations. These techniques may come under the knife of Congress by imposition of minimum and maximum terms for GRATs. Current proposals include a requirement that a GRAT have a minimum ten-year term and a maximum term of no more than ten years over the grantor's life expectancy, a requirement that the remainder interest be at least equal to 25 percent of the value of the assets contributed or $500,000, and a prohibition against tax-free exchanges of assets held in the trust. Passage of these proposals would make it impossible to structure a GRAT so that no taxable gift is made. (Read further about the current advantages of GRATs later in this chapter.)

‣ **Generation-skipping transfer tax (GST) exemption to be capped at 90 years.** This could effectively limit GST planning opportunities to 90 years, as opposed to potentially continuing trusts "in perpetuity." The cap would serve to subject assets to the reach of the IRS to tax repeatedly through the generations.

‣ **Grantor trusts could be included in the grantor's estate (the person who made the gift).** This could affect all types of grantor trusts.

‣ **Other negative impacts.** We could see limitation or exclusion of the following:

  • Family income trusts (FITs)

  • Sales to intentionally defective income trusts (IDITs)

  • Spousal lifetime access trusts (SLATs)

  • Irrevocable life insurance trusts (ILITs)

Clearly, it is advantageous to transfer wealth to these trusts sooner, rather than later, before assets appreciate. Also, do it before interest rates and valuations climb.

On the income tax front, some of the deductions at risk include mortgage interest deductions, limits on charitable contributions, and an overall cap on itemized deductions. When it comes to future tax law changes, everything is on the table. The government is on the prowl for revenue. Take advantage of these "endangered species" techniques before they are extinct.

Family Income Trust (FIT)

Rather than making gifts outright to family members, you might consider a family income trust (FIT), also known as a "family bank" or an irrevocable trust, as a receptacle of gifts. The terms and conditions of

> **A trust may be thought of as a "box with instructions."**

the trust, including income and principal distributions, can be flexible and may be tailored to your distribution goals. Additionally, the family income trust can ensure that assets left to your children will be protected and stay within your family bloodline.

A trust may be thought of as a "box with instructions." You place assets inside the box with instructions on the outside as to how your future heirs should open or close the box and when. Instructions may be left to:

- Your spouse—while you're alive and after you're gone
- Your children—while you and your spouse are alive and after you're both gone
- Your grandchildren—while you and your children are alive and after all of you are gone

This is often preferable to giving assets outright to family members. A family income trust can do the following:

- Provide liquidity to pay estate taxes by purchasing assets from the taxable estate
- Direct loan proceeds to the estate in order to pay taxes
- Make distributions to heirs to support their lifestyle, buy a house, start a business, educate grandchildren, etc.
- Equalize inheritances
- Protect assets from creditors, liability, divorce, and taxes
- Provide the trustee the use of gifted cash to acquire life insurance on the trust grantor(s) (this is a highly efficient method to provide for future payment of estate taxes)

Advantages

The advantages of a FIT include the following:

- It protects gifted assets from creditors and predators of trust beneficiaries.

- It receives assets transferred through the use of annual exclusion and lifetime gift tax exemptions.

- It removes assets from estate taxation at the death of the grantor.

- Certain trusts, such as SLATs, allow the trustee access to trust assets to make distributions of income to the nongrantor spouse. In other words, assets can be transferred outside of the taxable estate, but there is still access to the assets, if needed. You can have your cake and eat it too!

- It removes growth of gifted assets from the estate.

- It provides management assistance for beneficiaries.

- It provides a fund of cash that can be used to loan money to or purchase assets from a decedent's estate, thereby creating estate tax liquidity.

- I distributes principal and income to beneficiaries without the use of additional exclusion or credits through an independent trustee.

- It avoids probate.

Considerations

When considering these techniques, remember the following:

- In general, a trust that is irrevocable cannot be changed. However, the trust can be drafted to provide for flexibility in case of changing tax laws or personal circumstances through special "kick-out" distribution provisions for the beneficiaries and trust-to-trust merger provisions. Sometimes assets in an existing trust can be "decanted" or transferred into a new trust with different provisions.

- You usually will lose control over assets to the chosen trustee once they are transferred into the trust (unless a SLAT).

- To qualify for the annual gift tax exclusion, the trust should provide its beneficiaries with the right to withdraw gifts from the trust for a certain time (typically 30 days) after the gifts are made. These withdrawal powers are known as Crummey powers. By the way, if you already have an FIT, has the trustee sent *Crummey* notices to all beneficiaries each year a gift was made?

Using Single Life Insurance and/or Second-to-Die (Survivorship) Life Insurance in a FIT

Your family income trust (FIT) could be the owner and beneficiary of life insurance to pay estate taxes. Consider issuing policies for either one or both spouses if married. (To review the many other ways in which life insurance plays a role in your One Way Out, see chapter 6, "Protecting Your Business with Life Insurance.")

Advantages

The advantages of single life insurance are as follows:

- It creates an additional security blanket for the surviving spouse and family in the event of a premature death. If, through present value analysis of objectives and resources, it is determined that a need exists for additional capital upon the death of a family member, then, clearly, the use of single life insurance is indicated.

- The proceeds of a single life policy inside an ILIT will be received when the insured dies. Those proceeds can be invested inside the ILIT for growth. Depending on when the surviving spouse passes away, the estate may have experienced substantial growth by the time estate taxes are due.

- A SLAT may own single life insurance. This provides access to cash value for the nongrantor spouse during his or her lifetime.

Second-to-Die (Survivorship) Insurance

This form of insurance has several potential advantages:

- It helps pay the ultimate estate taxes due on second death through utilization of the unlimited marital deduction and tax deferral. The survivorship insurance premium is usually 40 percent to 50 percent less than single life coverage.

- It absorbs an uninsurable (or highly rated) spouse combined with a healthy spouse to acquire cost-effective insurance.

- It can be extremely efficient and provide greater bang for the buck from a cash flow and gift tax (and GST exemption allocation) standpoint.

As part of a review of your wealth preservation plan, be sure to consider the use of both single life and survivorship insurance. Existing policies should be reviewed carefully. In some instances, cash value in existing single life policies can be liberated and reallocated toward the acquisition of second-to-die policies.

PHASE 4—ADVANCED PLANNING

Taking your planning to the next phase will allow you to effectively manage extremely high-net-worth estate tax problems.

After addressing phases 1, 2, and 3, what are high-net-worth families to do? They can't give away enough assets to manage their estate tax problem, but they *can* look at giving away the *best parts* of an asset.

Simply stated, an asset can be divided into two parts: income interest and a remainder interest. With certain strategies, you can retain the income interest—that is, the right to receive income (such as rents, interest, and dividends) from an asset—but at the end of a certain number of years, the asset itself (reminder interest), plus growth, passes to a family member or trust for his or her benefit, free of any gift or estate taxes.

On Wall Street and in the financial markets, these kinds of transactions are sometimes called *arbitrage transactions*. In wealth preservation, they are usually called grantor retained annuity trust (GRAT), qualified personal residence trust (QPRT), or intentionally defective irrevocable trust (IDIT) sales. Each involves the same basic concept: transferring an asset (hopefully for less than full price) for future payments at a given rate of interest. In practice, each of these transactions seeks to reduce estate taxes by transferring value and growth.

Generation-Skipping Transfer (GST) Tax Planning

ATRA of 2012 extends the GST tax that was set to expire at the end of 2012. It affects transfers to your grandchildren, future grandchildren, and beyond. The exemption is now indexed for inflation and stands at $5.45 million per donor ($10.9 million per couple) for 2016, just like the gift and estate tax exemptions.

This creates extremely valuable immediate planning opportunities. In many instances, you and your spouse can use your GST exemptions to shelter $10.9 million (or more with advanced planning techniques) of your family wealth from estate, gift, and GST taxes—not just at your children's deaths but *forever.*

Thus, proper planning of gifts and bequests to take advantage of the fact that the GST has been made permanent allows many families to achieve long-term tax savings of tens of millions of dollars. It allows them to shift great wealth to multigenerational and dynasty trusts with asset protection features.

ATRA of 2012 has eliminated the uncertainty surrounding the GST and other estate tax provisions, thus making them "permanent." However, even that is a relative term. As I write this, a revenue-hungry Congress and administration are already looking to limit the duration of the GST exemption.

For now, GST exemptions are a valuable wealth preservation tool. However, beware the "automatic allocation" rule, which means that many people are unknowingly wasting their GST exemptions by making gifts to nondynasty (GST) trusts. A thorough review of your gift-giving history and gift tax returns filed should be undertaken to properly plan for the use of your precious GST exemption.

Grantor Retained Annuity Trust (GRAT)

A GRAT is an irrevocable trust into which you (the grantor) place assets and retain an annuity (income stream) for a fixed period of years. At the end of the specified period of years, the principal will pass to your beneficiary, such as your child or another trust for his or her benefit. During this period, the trustee will pay the donor/grantor (you) either a fixed amount with a GRAT or a fixed percentage of the value of the asset with a GRUT (grantor retained unitrust) on an annual basis by using trust income and, if necessary, principal. If the grantor survives the term of years, all GRAT assets are out of the grantor's estate.

A gift is made to your beneficiaries upon creation of the trust. But since the trust principal will not be distributed to your beneficiaries (usually your children) immediately, the Internal Revenue Code permits a discount on the gift. GRATs work best in a low-interest-rate environment—like the one we are in right now.

IDIT (Intentionally Defective Income Trust)

An IDIT sale is the "sale" of an asset for a promissory note. It is a sale, rather than a gift, to a trust. However, a separate gift is typically made to the trust equivalent to 10 percent of the value of the asset sold to the trust as seed money.

You (as grantor) can create a trust for the benefit of your family. The trust (IDIT) is designed so that assets owned by the trust will be out of your taxable estate but any taxable income generated by the trust will be taxed back to you as the grantor. The trust could then purchase income-producing, appreciating property from you in exchange for an interest-bearing installment note (or interest-only note with a balloon principal).

As grantor trusts are on the government's "endangered species list," act now to implement a sale to an IDIT while you still can, and hopefully Congress will pass liberal grandfathering provisions.

Benefits

An IDIT offers several benefits:

- No gain or loss is recognized on the sale to the trust.
- All income, gains, losses, and deductions flow through to the grantor. Thus, the grantor is taxed on trust income but not taxed separately on the interest received on the note.
- Appreciation of assets in the trust is not included in the grantor's taxable estate.
- Significant generation-skipping opportunities exist.
- Interest can be as low as the applicable federal rate (AFR).

Valuation Discounts

Many high-net-worth individuals understand that in business, the sum is greater than the parts—and the same holds true in estate preservation. For instance, voting stock is worth more than nonvoting stock (because control is better than no control). Additionally, half a beach house is worth less than 50 percent of the market value of the entire house, because sharing means losing complete control, and that sharing penalty should be reflected in how much is paid for the right to share.

In planning parlance, these attributes (partial ownership, unequal control, and lack of marketability) are called *valuation discounts*. Since the object of tax planning is often to decrease value for tax purposes, advanced estate preservation strategies often involve voluntarily breaking things apart (creating minority ownership), locking them down (removing marketability), or surrendering power (creating nonvoting interests) so that more value is preserved for your family.

Family Limited Partnership (FLP) or Family Limited Liability Company (FLLC) with Minority Interest Discounts

Another area to explore would be the structuring of assets into an FLP or FLLC, in order to realize discounts on current gift and future estate tax liability. Valuation discounts claimed on transfers to related parties are on the government's "endangered species list." Act quickly, as this ability to claim discounts may not exist in future years. Consolidating ownership and management of family assets and shifting future appreciation to other family members also help.

How to Implement

- ▶ Create an FLP or FLLC.
- ▶ Transfer assets (such as income-producing real estate or marketable securities) to the FLP or FLLC.
- ▶ Gift limited partners' (LPs') interests to family members; retain general partners' (GPs') interests (with an LLC, similar terms are "managing" and "nonmanaging" members).

Advantages

- ▶ General partner retains control.
- ▶ Gift taxes are reduced through discounting.
- ▶ Forming the FLP or FLLC is relatively simple.
- ▶ The partnership (or operating) agreement is flexible and amendable.
- ▶ Income shifting is possible.
- ▶ FLP or FLLC interests may have some protection from creditors under state law.

For example, if you isolate $15 million of assets in excess of exemption, and assume that it will double in value between today and the time of your death 12 years from now (though I hope that your prospects are much better!), you could have a tax liability of $10.5 million (on that $30 million at 40 percent). Conversely, if you transfer the $15 million of assets into an FLP today, and claim a minority interest discount of approximately 35 percent, the gift is not $15 million but only $10 million, with no gift tax required.

This technique includes further discounts for lack of voting control and illiquidity. If you again assume that this investment asset doubles in value to $30 million, then at your death, only $10 million is subject to tax (the discounted value when gifted), and $20 million escapes taxation. This results in a tax savings of $8 million ($20 million at 40 percent).

Mixing and Matching

FLPs and FLLCs could also be combined with other techniques, such as GRATs, sales to an IDIT, and other advanced strategies.

PHASE 5—CHARITABLE PLANNING (WITH ZERO ESTATE TAX)

If you find it consistent with your family values, you can transfer an unlimited number of assets to qualifying charitable organizations during your lifetime or at death without paying any gift or estate taxes. Income tax savings also apply for lifetime contributions. Following are five of the most effective charitable giving techniques.

Outright Gifts to Charity

Charitable gifts that you make directly to a charity during your lifetime will qualify for an income tax deduction. Note that this deduction may be limited in a single tax year if it exceeds certain percentages of your adjusted gross income (AGI).

For example, your deduction may be limited to 20 percent, 30 percent, or 50 percent of AGI, depending on whether you contribute cash or other property and the type of entity receiving the gift. However, you may be able to use the excess deduction as a carryforward for the following five tax years.

The PATH ACT of 2015 permanently extended a special provision for IRA charitable rollovers. Taxpayers who are 70½ or older can donate up to $100,000 directly from their IRAs to qualified charities without having to account for the distributions as taxable income, and these distributions are not subject to AGI limitations. Therefore, such a donation will be fully tax-deductible.

Charitable Remainder Trusts

You can also establish a charitable remainder trust (CRT) during your lifetime or upon your death. You can transfer an asset to a lifetime CRT, and retain the right to receive payments from it for a certain period of time. This can be either a specified number of years or, if you desire, for your lifetime and over your spouse's lifetime. Upon death, the assets remaining in the CRT will be transferred to one or more charities you designate.

A CRT can be particularly attractive if you have assets, such as closely held business interests (e.g., non-pass-through entities), publicly traded stocks, or real estate, that have appreciated significantly over your basis. The benefits of a CRT include the following:

- Avoidance (or deferral) of capital gains tax upon disposition of the contributed asset
- Charitable income tax deduction based on the actuarial fair-market remainder value of assets contributed to the trust
- Reduced estate taxes
- Potentially increased income stream (100 cents of a dollar to invest, not reduced by income tax on sale of the asset)
- Substantial benefit to the charity/charities of your choosing

Charitable Lead Trusts

Another popular vehicle for those who wish to make current gifts to charity is a charitable lead trust (CLT). A CLT is essentially the opposite of a CRT. It provides an income stream to a charity during your life or for a specified period of time. After the trust term ends or upon death, the remaining trust assets pass to the donor or to family beneficiaries named in the trust.

Private Foundations

You can also consider establishing a private foundation and funding it with appreciated assets, cash, or life insurance. Contributions to private foundations are eligible for an income tax deduction (subject to certain income and type of property contributed limitations). Most foundations are required to pay out a percentage of their income each year to charity. Family members can be involved as trustees of the foundation and can earn reasonable fees for their time and efforts in its management and selection of worthy charities.

Charitable Planning Coupled with Wealth Replacement Trusts

Even those with strong charitable inclinations can often feel that although the IRS is not receiving the assets directed to charity (which is a very good thing), their families are also not receiving them. To ameliorate this concern, they often establish a wealth replacement trust to replace the assets going to charity. Often, charitable techniques—CRTs, CLTs, private foundations—are coupled with an FIT, or irrevocable family income trust, sometimes referred to as a wealth replacement trust.

In fact, the grantor can use a portion of the cash received from income tax savings, or the income stream retained in the case of a CRT, to make gifts to the wealth replacement trust. The trustee can then purchase life insurance on one or both donors to benefit the family and replace some or all of the assets passing to charity.

CHAPTER SUMMARY

Estate planning and wealth preservation is a necessary part of your holistic One Way Out plan. The threat of the IRS forcing liquidation of 40 percent of your net worth, or potential attacks from predators and creditors seeking to confiscate dollars from you or your family, is a motivation.

A wealth preservation plan will help accomplish your objectives in the following areas:

- Providing for your surviving spouse and other family members in the event of your demise.
- Providing that assets will be managed properly if you become disabled or incompetent.
- Distributing your assets, including your business if you own it at the time of your death, in accordance with your wishes.
- Protecting assets from predators and creditors.
- Maximizing use of all applicable Internal Revenue Code deductions, exclusions, and tax credits to save taxes.
- Making sure that your family pays the minimum amount of income, gift, estate, and generation-skipping taxes.
- Ensuring that your charitable intentions are met.
- Providing for an equitable distribution of assets among your children.
- Objectively reviewing your existing legal documents, such as wills, trusts, powers of attorney, living wills, health-care directives, prenuptial agreements, divorce decrees, and the like.
- Reviewing the ownership and beneficiary designation of life insurance policies and qualified retirement plans to minimize tax consequences and make sure they flow to whom you want, when you want, and in the proper amounts.
- Developing a prearranged plan for the management and expenses associated with long-term care.

Begin by reviewing your current estate plan, particularly if you have family involved in your business or if you have experienced major life events such as a marriage, divorce, or birth of a child or grandchild. Also review will and trust provisions for formulas that may no longer accurately reflect your dispositive wishes. To help make the wealth preservation process as efficient as possible, proceed in phases:

- **Fundamental:** Making sure your estate documents accomplish your objectives and are up-to-date. This includes your (and your spouse's) wills, trusts, powers of attorney, living wills, health care agents, asset titling, IRA beneficiary designations, and life insurance ownership and beneficiary designations.

- **Basic:** Taking advantage of the gift tax annual exclusion, currently $14,000 per year ($28,000 for a married couple) per beneficiary. Gifts of cash, business interests, or other property may be given outright or into trusts for estate tax savings and asset protection.

- **Intermediate:** Executing the lifetime utilization of a portion or all of the $5.45 million gift tax exemption ($10.9 million per couple) in 2016, indexed for inflation. This allows you to transfer assets out of your taxable estate so that future appreciation escapes estate and generation-skipping transfer taxes (GST).

- **Advanced:** For very large estates, consider the gift or sale of a remainder interest. Techniques such as a GRAT, QPRT, FLP, FLLC, or sale to an IDIT are extremely effective for reducing estate taxes.

- **Charitable planning:** If your goal is to make gifts during your lifetime or at your death to charities, you can make outright gifts, or establish a charitable remainder trust, charitable lead trust, or private foundation.

You choose how far along this planning process you wish to go. Keep in mind that many strategies available today are on the "endangered species list," and may not survive the next round of tax changes designed to raise revenue. By acting now, you can take advantage of current techniques such as the following:

- Short- and long-term GRATs

- Grantor trusts used for estate planning purposes

- Valuation discounts on family wealth transfers

- Generation-skipping planning before duration is capped at 90 years

I encourage you to be proactive and learn about the various techniques, their pros and cons, and how they may apply to your family's needs. Getting lost in the technical jargon is easy, so find someone who can explain everything in terms to which you can relate. It doesn't need to be complicated to be effective.

Then, decide which to implement and *do it!* Acting now could avoid millions of dollars lost to taxes or exposed to other threats by transferring your wealth to those you care about most: your family and possibly charitable causes. Then and only then, in conjunction with the other strategies described in this book, will you be well positioned to take optimal advantage of your One Way Out!

Download the Wealth Planning checklist at <u>YourOneWayOut.com</u>.

PrisCo Financial Resources and Services

To SERVE THE NEEDS OF OUR CLIENTELE, PrisCo Financial has access to specialized resources and services to provide a comprehensive client experience to help them achieve their optimal One Way Out.

- ▶ Holistic financial planning, wealth accumulation, family business succession, and wealth preservation provided through **Sagemark Consulting Private Wealth Services (SCPWS).**

- ▶ For owners who desire to protect and grow their businesses prior to their exit, we utilize the **Business Intelligence Institute (BII).**

- ▶ For owners who are ready to exit and choose a sale of their business to either a strategic buyer, financial buyer, management buyout, ESOP, or IPO, we have access to M&A and investing banking talent through **Equity Strategies Group (ESG).**

SAGEMARK CONSULTING PRIVATE WEALTH SERVICES

Sagemark Consulting Private Wealth Services (SCPWS) is an essential resource for financial planners, who are classified among an elite group within the Lincoln Financial Advisors organization nationwide. Dan Prisciotta is affiliated with this elite group that specializes in working with wealthy families

Our resources
through Lincoln Financial Advisors

- Access to firm-wide
  Planning Resources
- National Design Legal Staff
- Advanced Estate Planning
- Wealth Preservation
- Retirement / Financial
  Independence Planning
- Financial Condition Model
- Risk Management Analysis
- Life Insurance Strategies
- Asset Protection
- Income Tax Reduction

- Tax-Exempt Dynasty Trusts
- Disability / Long Term Care
- Charitable Planning
- Investment Portfolio
- Review & Design
- Asset Allocation
  – Managed Assets
  – Mutual Funds
  – ETFs
- IRA Optimization
- Guaranteed Income
- Annuities

- Company Sponsored
  Qualified Retirement
  Plans
  – Profit Sharing
  – 401(k)
  – Defined Benefit
- Education Funding
- Oil & Gas Tax Programs
- Real Estate / REITS
- PIG / PAL Matching

BUSINESS INTELLIGENCE INSTITUTE

BUSINESS OWNER PLANNING
- Growth Strategies
- Owner & Executive
  Compensation Planning
- Non-Qualified Deferred
  Compensation Plans
- Corporate Tax Strategies
- Split Dollar Design
- Key Person Solutions
- Family Succession
- Buy / Sell Agreements
- Corporate Policy Review
- Group Insurance
- Synthetic Equity Plans
  – Phantom Stock Plan
  – Stock Grant Plans
  – SAR Plans
  – Stock Option Plans

ESG
Equity Strategies Group

M&A & INVESTMENT BANKING SERVICES
- Sale of Business to:
  – Strategic Buyer
  – Private Equity
  – Management Team
  – ESOP
- Pre-Sale Tax Planning
- Business Valuation
- Marketability Assessments
- Value Gap Analysis
- Business Exit Readiness
  Index (BERI)
- Access to Capital
- Private Equity
- Recapitalization
- Debt Refinancing

in the $10 million-plus net worth marketplace. SCPWS supports its financial planners to provide the highest quality case design and overall value to this specific market segment. SCPWS offers their membership of financial planners the following services:

- ▶ By utilizing the expertise of the SCPWS staff, PrisCo Financial is able to deliver a consortium-level approach to its clients' financial needs.

- ▶ Along with the talent of SCPWS, PrisCo Financial develops strategies and tangible, implementable solutions. Throughout the process, you will have the opportunity to interact with any one of these internal resources, as needed. Your financial situation will be handled by a a qualified, credentialed, and competent group of professinals who stand ready to discuss and illustrate their recommendations in real time.

- ▶ As a successful business person, you are, by nature, a person of action. At SCPWS we believe that a financial plan in and of itself has no power or force without implementable actions that change your situation in a way that appropriately helps you toward your goals. Our action orientation drives us to deliver to you multiple options, which we then can assist you in implementing. Each generates a quantifiable outcome. You are the judge of your own destiny, but we will give you the tools to decide your fate both today and in the future.

- ▶ We value your business and will cater to your needs and requests in a manner that earns your respect. Our response will be timely, efficient, and dependable. Throughout the financial planning process, you can count on us to drive at a pace that is appropriate to your particular situation and needs. Our relationship will evolve, as will your financial plan, but you will always be treated to a timely, concierge-level experience from complex issue to minute detail.

BUSINESS INTELLIGENCE INSTITUTE (BII)

The Business Intelligence Institute (BII) is a national initiative focused on serving the needs of closely held business owners to help them grow, preserve, protect, and transfer their life's work. Dan Prisciotta is the co-founder, along with his partner, Jack McCaughan. They are the creative force behind BII, and introduced the concept to Lincoln Financial Advisors. Dan is a thought leader involved in shaping the training program, process, and deliverables to clients and advisors selected for participation in BII. Only the most highly qualified professionals within Lincoln Financial Advisors are invited to participate in this effort. Our mission is to utilize our holistic business planning process, culture, and intellectual capital to help our entrepreneurial clients make informed choices toward reaching their business and personal goals. We work with owners to accomplish the following:

- Show them how to protect and grow their business in the years leading up to their exit
- Help determine the value of their business for planning purposes
- Create a roadmap to help increase the value of their business by emphasis on value drivers
- Recognize their best succession or exit path, whether internally or externally, i.e., discover their best One Way Out
- Transfer ownership as profitably and tax efficiently as possible
- Create a contingency plan in the event they, or their partners or key employees, do not survive until their business exit is completed
- Help businesses attract, retain, and incentivize key management personnel
- Integrate personal, financial, and wealth preservation goals with the goals of their business to maximize profit and minimize tax liabilities

EQUITY STRATEGIES GROUP (ESG)

Dan Prisciotta is the founder and managing partner of Equity Strategies Group (ESG). ESG has regional offices representing the New York metro area, New England, the mid-Atlantic, and the western United States, with coverage in all 50 states. ESG's focus is the design and implementation of successful exit strategies for owners who have determined that an immediate sale of their business is their ideal One Way Out. We serve our clients by helping to clarify and meet their exit strategy goals while adhering to the highest standards of professionalism and integrity.

With nearly 12 million business owners approaching a stage in their lives when a business exit is on the near horizon, ESG provides a total solution to help meet their needs. In addition to creating marketability assessments and business value driver assessments, we provide an integrated platform of services through our alliance with twenty of the premier middle-market investment banks and M&A firms in the United States to help implement select investment banking transactions:

- ◗ Sale of a business
- ◗ Private equity recapitalization
- ◗ Mergers and acquisitions
- ◗ Raising capital for growth and expansion
- ◗ Management buyouts
- ◗ Employee stock ownership plans (ESOPs)
- ◗ Refinancing

YOUR ONE WAY OUT SUCCESS STARTS HERE

As the owner of a closely held business, you're often too busy "fighting alligators" to give the future its full due. Yet, your ultimate success will be measured by the creation and implementation of a comprehensive business and personal plan that improves the probability of attaining your vision, values, and goals. To that end, we offer a full range of services:

- ◗ **Clear, understandable guidance.** We listen carefully, analyze fully, and then provide recommendations that are relevant, timely, and—above all—understandable.

- ◗ **Custom solutions.** We provide confidential, highly customized solutions that emphasize you and your needs—not a prepackaged set of solutions or ideas.

- ◗ **A complete wealth management experience specifically designed for business owners.** Our work both supplements and coordinates the services of your existing team of advisors, such as a trusted attorney or accountant. In addition, we are experienced in marshalling the resources of our nationwide network available through Lincoln Financial Advisors, Sagemark Consulting Private Wealth Services, Business Intelligence Institute, and Equity Strategies Group to provide you with a holistic planning process to help you achieve success.

- ◗ **A close, personal, consultative relationship built on trust and understanding.** Business owner planning is not a static event. Your strategies are regularly reviewed to ensure they remain consistent with your long-term objectives and are aligned with our ever-changing world. Through it all, we keep you at the center of the process.

"Serve First, Last, and Always^{SM}" is our overriding philosophy—the one that uniquely defines the way we do business. We are your advocates.

Index

Note: Page numbers with *f* represent figures. Page numbers with *t* represent tables.

G

I

Disclaimer/Disclosure

THIS PUBLICATION IS DESIGNED to provide information about the subject matter covered. It is sold with the understanding that while the author is a financial advisor and registered representative, he, his firm, and the publisher are not engaged by the reader to render legal, accountant, or other professional service. The purpose of this book is to educate. Neither the author, nor Sagemark Consulting Private Wealth Services, nor Lincoln Financial Advisors, nor Equity Strategies Group, nor Daniel A. Prisciotta, shall have any liability or responsibility to any person or entity with respect to any loss or damage caused, or alleged to be caused, directly or indirectly by the information contained in this book. If you do not wish to be found by the above, you may return this book to the publisher for a full refund.

Lincoln Financial Advisors Corporation and its representatives do not provide legal or tax advice. You may want to consult a legal or tax advisor regarding any legal or tax information as it relates to your personal circumstances.

Securities offered through Lincoln Financial Advisors Corporation, a broker/dealer. Equity Strategies Group is the marketing name used to reflect specialized planning strategies and techniques. Investment advisory services offered through Sagemark Consulting, a division of Lincoln Financial Advisors Corporation, a registered investment advisor. Insurance offered through Lincoln Affiliates and other fine companies.

Prisco Financial is not an affiliate of Lincoln Financial Advisors. We provide critical, team attention for your financial planning needs that is difficult to match anywhere else.

CREDITS

Publisher/Editorial Director: Michael Roney

Art Director: Sarah M. Clarehart

Copyeditor: Sandra Judd

Proofreader: Amanda Price

Indexer: Karl Ackley

Contact: info@highpointpubs.com

HIGHPOINT
EXECUTIVE
PUBLISHING

www.highpointpubs.com